Teachable Transitions

Teachable Transitions

190 Activities to Move from Morning Circle to the End of the Day

Rae Pica

gryphon house
Beltsville, MD

Dedication

This book is dedicated to my mother, Eleanor Pica-Merrill, for her steadfast love and for the pride in me that she never fails to display.

Acknowledgments

I'd like to offer my gratitude to my editor, Kathy Charner, for being such a pleasure to work with—and to everyone at Gryphon House. I'm delighted to be a member of the family! Special thanks to Leah Curry-Rood for her part in bringing me into the clan.

Author Availability

Rae Pica is internationally known for her workshops and presentations on movement's role in children's lives and education. To arrange for staff development training, conference workshops, or keynote speeches, contact her through Gryphon House, PO Box 207, Beltsville, MD 20704-0207 or at raepica@movingandlearning.com.

Copyright 2003 © Rae Pica

Published by Gryphon House, Inc., 10726 Tucker Street, Beltsville, MD 20705 or P.O. Box 207, Beltsville, MD 20704-0207.
(800) 638-0928, (301) 595-9500, (301) 595-0051 (Fax)

Visit us on the web at www.gryphonhouse.com

Illustrations: Kathy Dobbs

Bulk purchase

Gryphon House books are available for special premiums and sales promotions as well as for fund-raising use. Special editions or book excerpts also can be created to specification. For details, contact the Director of Marketing at the address above.

Disclaimer

Gryphon House, Inc. and the author cannot be held responsible for damage, mishap, or injury incurred during the use of or because of activities in this book. Appropriate and reasonable caution and adult supervision of children involved in activities and corresponding to the age and capability of each child involved, is recommended at all times. Do not leave children unattended at any time. Observe safety and caution at all times.

Library of Congress Cataloging-in-Publication Data

Pica, Rae, 1953-
   Teachable transitions: 190 activities to move from morning circle to the end of the day / Rae Pica; illustrations, Kathy Dobbs-
      p. cm.
   Includes index.
   ISBN 0-87659-281-7
   1. Early childhood education-Activity programs. 2. Movement education. 3. Classroom management I- Title,
LB1139.35.A37P53 2003
372.21--dc21   2002151263

Table of Contents

Introduction

Teachable Transitions: 190 Activities to Move from Morning Circle to the End of the Day will help you move children from one area of your classroom or school or one time of day to another. The activities, which include games, songs, and chants, are designed to help children learn to bring satisfactory closure to activities, to move easily into and out of group situations, and to hold their attention while waiting for their turn. The activities are so enjoyable that you may find that children look forward to daily transitions. The activities will also help children learn to follow directions "from the simple to the complex and concerned with locations, object descriptions, and sequences of actions" (Allen & Hart, 1984, p. 104). Because these activities are organized by time of day and many are linked to traditional themes, they can be easily integrated into the curriculum, so they add continuity and more opportunity for learning to the day's components.

The transitions in this book offer children valuable learning experiences, including the chance to review something experienced previously in the day or week. For example, they can demonstrate that they remember a movement that they learned earlier in the day, or they can move from one situation to another the same way as a character in a favorite book they read earlier.

Many of the activities reinforce popular classroom themes. Activities connected to specific themes have icons that help you locate them at a glance. The activities focus on language arts and music through chants, poems, and songs. In addition, the cooperative group activities build a sense of community and provide important practice in social studies as children learn about themselves and others.

Opportunities abound for problem solving, creativity, and self-expression throughout *Teachable Transitions*. Divergent problem solving—where there are many possible responses to a single challenge is a skill that is important to creative and critical thinking. Children can imagine solutions to problems and challenges. They can imagine what it is like to be someone or something else. They can imagine answers to the question, "What if?" And they can plan full and satisfying futures. For all of these reasons, many of the transitions in this book give children a chance to use their imaginations.

Finally, the activities in *Teachable Transitions* offer experiences with movement and music. The majority of the activities involve some kind of movement, either in place (stationary) or moving (traveling). You can also use transition times to practice a previously learned movement. For example, as children move from place to place, they may be asked to perform their favorite movement that they learned earlier in the day, or to execute a specific movement skill, such as galloping (locomotor), turning (nonlocomotor), or pretending to pull something (manipulative).

When children sing as encouraged by the activities in *Teachable Transitions* and go about their daily actions, they experience the musical elements of pitch, tempo, and rhythm. The notion of music as an integral part of daily life becomes ingrained.

Using This Book

Planning your transitions with the contents of *Teachable Transitions* is easy. Because each chapter focuses on one daily transition, you simply choose one activity for each transition. Young children love and need repetition, so you can use the same activities for a period of time: one week, two weeks, or for as long as children continue to enjoy them and/or they are still effective.

Whenever possible, I have included variations for each activity. This will make the activities more effective for a longer period of time and children will have the benefit of repetition and variety. Moreover, the modifications will keep the activities fresh for you.

Teaching Fingerplays, Songs, and Movement

When teaching fingerplays to children, follow the process outlined by Hamilton and Flemming (1990), who suggest that you first demonstrate the actions while speaking or singing the words. Then repeat the process, encouraging children to perform only the actions. On the next repetition, children who choose to can participate with both actions and words.

When teaching songs to children, repeat them as often as necessary, assuring children that you don't expect them to sing along until they feel comfortable doing so. Often, young children will not sing a song until it has become as familiar as an old friend.

When teaching movements, children should understand and respect the concept of personal space. They should not touch one another unless it is a specific part of the activity. You can explain the concept of personal space by asking children to imagine they are each inside their own giant bubble. Then have them practice moving without bursting anyone else's bubble!

General Tips

Of course, in addition to planning activities you want to use during the day, there are other things you can do to ensure smooth transitions. The following are a few general tips, excerpted from Pica (2000, pp. 263-264):

- Remain calm and collected. If you appear "unhinged" during transitions, children will become unhinged, too. On the other hand, if you move slowly and speak softly, they will respond in kind.
- Make necessary preparations in advance. If children are transitioning to lunch, for instance, they should not have to sit at the table waiting; the meal should be ready as children are concluding their prior activity. By the same token, if the transition itself involves a prop, or maybe a fingerplay, have it ready beforehand.
- If the transition involves taking turns, such as those involving toileting or donning outerwear, be sure the same children aren't always chosen to go first. Hildebrand (1980, p. 97) writes, "Children learn to wait their turns when they know from experience that they will get a turn." For example, one day you can assign brown-eyed children to go to the coatroom first. The next day all children wearing blue can go first, with children born in January asked to lead on the following day.

Ready, Set, Go

The format for the activities in *Teachable Transitions* is simple. It is *Ready, Set, Go!* In *Ready*, you will find background information you need about the activity. For example, this section will tell you if the activity has specific connections to a content area, and what children will learn by doing the activity.

Set tells you what you need to do to prepare children for the activity. Should they be standing in a circle? Are there concepts or directions they need to understand? Are there props that need to be set up? (To make the activities in *Teachable Transitions* easy to use, most require little or no materials; however, there are a few that require props.)

Go describes the activity and, if necessary, provides words to a song, chant, or fingerplay. Related ideas are presented under the heading *Another Transition Idea*.

Some experts suggest that transitions are an accumulation of wasted time (Davidson, 1982), but when you plan for transitions—just as other parts of the day are planned—you will ensure that they, too, offer children many and varied learning experiences.

Because typical transitions in the early childhood setting are part of each day—arrival, snacks and lunch, cleanup, rest or naptime, transitions to outside the classroom, and departure—you will find activities for all of these in *Teachable Transitions*.

Wishing you teachable transitioning!

Arrival

We all like to be welcomed because it makes us feel special. Teachers and caregivers can make the children in their program feel special—and get the day started right—by providing a warm welcome for each and every arriving child.

Especially warming is the sound of one's own name, which children love to hear. Simply saying, "Good morning (Tony)" may not be enough to generate enthusiasm and make the child feel glad to be there. Instead, as children arrive, meet them at the door and use the activities on pages 12-17 ("Good Morning to You" to "When I Grow Up"). The children will look forward to arriving each day!

In addition, this chapter contains activities you can do with children who have removed their outerwear and are ready to begin their day. These activities are on pages 17-22 ("Come Together" to "A Holiday Question"). Later, when everyone has finally arrived, use the activities from the third section of this chapter on pages 22-29 ("It's Time to Start Our Day" to "The Four Seasons") as a pleasant way to begin circle or group time, to create an atmosphere of unity, or to get ready for the day.

Finally, to transition into the rest of the day, it is always a good idea to talk with the children about what to expect that day and then perform a relevant song or movement activity. If you are focusing on a theme, relate it to the song or activity. For instance, if the theme is transportation, you might sing "Wheels on the Bus." You can then transition into the next part of the day by moving like any one of the many modes of transportation. Or, you can choose from one of the ideas on pages 29-34 ("Here We Go" to "Pass a Sound"), which include a number of activities appropriate for transitioning to whatever comes next in the day. You will find you can use many of these activities for other transitions within the classroom, as well.

Good Morning to You

Ready

- Use this simple welcoming song as you greet the children one-on-one at the door.
- The tune is a familiar one and the sentiment is simple, yet effective, for getting the day started on the right foot.

Set

- Look directly at the child as you sing.

Go

- Sing the following to the tune of "Happy Birthday."

    Good morning to you
    Good morning to you
    Good morning, dear (Kara),
    Good morning to you!

Here Today

Ready

- Here is another simple song with a favorite melody.

Set

- Smile and look directly at the child.

Go

- Sing the following to the tune of "London Bridge."

    (Catherine) is here today
    Here today, here today.
    (Catherine) is here today
    I'm (we're) so glad to see you!

Hello, Welcome

Ready

- This song uses the child's name *and* mentions the day of the week.
- Because it is longer than the previous two, you might choose this song on occasions when, in addition to greeting the children, you have to help them remove outerwear, or when you escort them to the center of the room.

Set

- Stress the day of the week or the child's name.

Go

- Sing the following to the tune of "Bicycle Built for Two" (also known as "Daisy").

> *Hello, welcome*
> *To (Keesha) on (Monday).*
> *I'm so glad to see you*
> *That's what I want to say!*
>
> *Hello, welcome*
> *To (Keesha) on this day.*
> *We're glad to have you with us.*
> *Won't you come in and play?*

Another Transition Idea

- If your weekly or monthly theme is *animals*, you can change the lyrics accordingly.

> *Hello, welcome*
> *To (Keesha) on this day.*
> *Our theme this week (month) is animals*
> *And how they live and play.*
>
> *So come in, join us*

As we learn all about
The world of different animals
We couldn't do without!

Hello to You

Ready

- Although this chant does not incorporate a child's name, you can still make it personal by preceding it with a hearty "Good morning" that uses the child's name.
- The handshake adds another personal touch. Children love to shake hands. It makes them feel grown up!

Set

- Recite this chant while shaking each child's hand.

Go

- Shake hands while saying, "How do you do?" and "Welcome to school!"

  Hello to you
  And how do you do?
  It's a wonderful morning—
  Welcome to school!

Another Transition Idea

- If you have a small number of children, use this chant with the group as a whole.
- Stand in a circle with the children and turn to the child on either your left or right. Shake hands with that child and recite the chant.
- That child then repeats the words and action with the next child in the circle, and so on, all the way around the circle.
- If you have a larger group, you can eliminate the hand-shaking and simply recite the chant together.

It's a Seasonal Thing

Ready

- Use this activity to move each child from the door to the group gathering or circle time area in the classroom.
- It will call attention to the season, give the child an opportunity to use self-expression and imagination, and make arrival fun!

Set

- Greet the child at the door and, if needed, help her remove outerwear.

Go

- Challenge the child to move from the door toward the rest of the children as though she were something related to the season; for example, a snowflake or snowperson in the wintertime, the breeze or the wind in spring, a falling leaf in fall, or the sun shining in summertime.

Another Transition Idea

- If there is a holiday approaching, modify this activity to address it.
- For instance, the children could move like a ghost for Halloween, a flag for Flag Day or another patriotic holiday, a flickering candle for Hanukkah, an elf for Christmas, and so on.

Hint: Assign the image or, when the children are developmentally ready, let them choose an image of their own.

Hello & Welcome

Ready

- Greet each arriving child with this little chant when a holiday or celebration is approaching.
- Because it is so brief, it is perfect when time is of the essence.

Set

- If the holiday or celebration is taking place that day, substitute the word *celebrate* for *look forward to.*
- Insert the name of the holiday.

Go

- The chant is as follows:

> *Hello and welcome*
> *We're glad you can be here.*
> *To look forward to (celebrate) (name of holiday or celebration)*
> *One of our favorite times of year!*

When I Grow Up

Ready

- Even if you are not exploring the theme of occupations with the children, this is a great activity for transitioning each child from the door to the group gathering in the classroom.
- This activity will get the creative and cognitive "juices" flowing and promote awareness of the valuable roles played by people in different lines of work.

Set

- Greet the child at the door and, if needed, help her remove outerwear.
- Ask her what she would like to be when she grows up.
- Once she has responded, ask for an example of a task performed by a person in that line of work.

Go

- Challenge the child to move from the door toward the rest of the children as though performing that particular task.
- For example, if one child indicated that she would like to be a basketball player, she might pretend to dribble a ball down the court. Or if another child said he wanted to be a teacher, he might pretend to write on a chalkboard as he joins his classmates.
- Challenge the children who have already gathered to guess the occupation that the arriving child is depicting.

Come Together

Ready

- Use this chant if several children are arriving at once and you want to call them together into a circle.
- They won't need much encouragement, as young children love to form a circle with their friends *and* they love the concept of taking a bow.

Set

- Explain what you expect of the children when you say the chant.

Go

- Be sure to use your most inviting voice when you chant the following rhyme.

> *Come together, come together*
> *Come together now.*
> *Stand together in a circle*
> *Take a great big bow!*

Good Morning, Good Morning

Ready
- Use this fingerplay with the group as a whole or with children who have arrived before the rest of the class.

Set
- Sit in a circle with the children.
- Suggestions for actions are at the end of each line of the poem.
- When spreading arms wide, be sure to cross them at the midline of the body before opening them up, as these movements are important to brain development.

Go
- Teach the children the following poem.

Good morning, good morning (clap-clap) (clap-clap)
Good morning to you. (spread arms wide)
I'm happy to be here. (trace shape of a smile with pointer finger)
I hope you're happy, too! (point at children; they point at you!)

How Are You This Fine Day?

Ready
- Sing this song as each child joins the group, or with all of the children sitting together in a circle.
- If the children are already in a circle, address one child at a time all the way around the circle.

Set
- Teach the children their parts and then sing the song.

Go

● Sing the following to the tune of "Where Is Thumbkin?"

Teacher: *How is (Maya)? How is (Maya)?*
Child: *I am fine. I am fine.*
Teacher: *We welcome you this (day of the week).*
We're glad to have you with us.
Children: *We're glad, too. We're glad, too.*

Show and Tell

Ready

- Children never tire of this age-old activity, which promotes language development and social skills.

Set

- The day before you do this activity, invite each child to bring something special to school the next day.
- Even if you have not done this, the children always have *something* with them, even if it is something they are wearing.

Go

- As each new arrival joins the circle, ask her to show something she brought or is wearing to school that day and to tell a little bit about it.

Guess What I Did

Ready

- This activity promotes communication and social skills.
- It also requires guessing, a form of problem solving that can help "wake up" the children's brains upon arrival!

Set

- Explain that one child will act out something she did the night before, and the other children have to guess what it is.

Go

- Each arriving child acts out something she did the night before, and the remaining children have to guess what it is.

How's the Weather?

Ready

- This chant calls the children's attention to the season and to the day's weather, which are science concepts.
- It also lends itself to any additional discussion you may have about the day, the season, or an upcoming holiday, which are social studies concepts.

Set

- Sit in a circle with the children for this chant.

Go

- You may accompany the chant by tapping a steady beat on your lap or on the floor in front of you.
- The chant is as follows:

> Good morning, good morning
> On this (winter's) day.
> The weather sure is (snowy; sunny; windy; cold)
> We're glad you're here today!

Another Transition Idea

- Once the children are familiar with this chant, you can ask them to provide the description of the day.
- Either they can each shout out a word, or you can point to a single child and let her supply it.
- Be sure to choose a different child each day!

A Holiday Question

Ready

- If a holiday is approaching, use this activity as each child arrives.

Set

- As each child arrives, ask her what first comes to her mind about the holiday or celebration in question.

Go

- Once the child has answered your question, ask her to show you her answer to depict the person or thing, or to act out the situation described.
- For example, if the child mentions a parade, invite a brief demonstration of what that looks like.
- If time permits, ask the rest of the children to join in the depiction.

It's Time to Start Our Day

Ready

- Create enthusiasm for the start of the day with this little song, sung to the tune of "Farmer in the Dell."

Set

- Sit in a circle with the children and teach them this song.

Go

- Explain that they should all shout "Hooray!" at the end of the song.
- The words to sing are:

  It's time to start our day.
  It's time to start our day.
  Let's give a great big cheer
  And then be on our way!
  Hooray!

- At the end of the song, tell them what they will be doing next and where to go in the classroom.

This Is My Friend

Ready

- When all the children have arrived and are gathered together, this activity (adapted from Orlick, 1978) is a wonderful way for teachers and children to welcome one another.

Set

- Stand in a circle with the children, holding hands.

Go

- Raise the arm of the child to your right or left, saying, "This is my friend...."
- That child then says her name, holds up the arm of the next person in the circle, and repeats, "This is my friend...."
- That child says her name and the process continues around the circle in the same direction until each child has introduced herself and all arms are in the air.
- Then all take a deep bow for a job well done.

Another Transition Idea

- Incorporate a seasonal focus by asking each child to follow her name with "...and my favorite thing about [season] is _____."

And Another Transition Idea

- Once the children know one another's names, they can introduce each other.
- For instance, upon raising the arm of the child to her right, Sarah might say, "This is my friend Jamal."
- After everyone has been introduced and all arms are in the air, everyone bows.

Hail, Hail

Ready

- This rousing song will get the children excited about being together as a group.

Set

- Sing this number to the tune of "Hail, Hail, the Gang's All Here" a couple of times through, several days in a row.
- The children will join you in no time.
- If you'd rather, change the informal "gonna," to the more proper "going to."

Go

- Sing the song and have fun!

  Hail, hail, the gang's all here.
  We're gonna have a good day.
  We're gonna learn while we play.
  Hail, hail, the gang's all here.
  We're gonna have a good time now!

Another Transition Idea

- Make this song a fingerplay by adding simple actions.
- Suggestions appear in brackets following each line.

> *Hail, hail, the gang's all here.* (two big waves of the hand; then indicate everyone gathered in the circle)
> *We're gonna have a good day.* (nod twice)
> *We're gonna learn while we play.* (tap the temple with the pointer finger twice)
> *Hail, hail, the gang's all here.* (repeat actions for first line)
> *We're gonna have a good time now!* (draw an invisible smile in front of face with pointer finger; nod twice.)

- Add a cheer at the end, fist raised to ceiling!

We're So Glad to Be Here

Ready

- This simple, four-line song and the discussion that follows it can set the stage for a great day.

Set

- Sit in a circle with the children.

Go

- Sing the following to the tune of "On Top of Old Smokey."

> *We're so glad to be here*
> *To see everyone.*
> *We're going to learn new things*
> *While we have some fun!*

- After singing the song through once or twice, go around the circle, asking the children, in turn, what they are most looking forward to doing that day.

Call-and-Response

Ready

- Children love call-and-response activities because it makes them feel like a part of something, and that's always a good way to start a day.

Set

- Sit in a circle with the children and explain what is going to happen.
- When you first begin to use this activity, you will have to provide the children with their responses, but it won't take many repetitions before they can respond on their own!

Go

- Follow the script below or feel free to make one up of your own!

> Teacher: Hi, everyone!
> Children: Hi!
> Teacher: How are you today?
> Children: Fine, thank you.
> Teacher: Do you know what day it is?
> Children: It's (Monday)!
> Teacher: Are you ready to have some fun?
> Children: Ycs!
> Teacher: Are you ready to learn something new?
> Children: Yes!
> Teacher: Then, how about we start our day?
> Children: Yea!

- Everyone applauds.
- Sing a song, say a fingerplay, or introduce the day's theme or objectives in another way.

Stand Up/Sit Down

Ready

- This activity gets both the brain and the body warmed up, while also working on the concepts of up and down.
- The children will think it's very funny!

Set

- Sit with the children, who are either in a circle or scattered throughout the space.

Go

- Invite the children to alternately stand up or sit down if:

  - they're glad to be there
  - they're feeling good that day
  - they're happy to see their friends
  - they're happy to see their teacher
  - they're looking forward to learning something new

- If the children are going to move to another area of the room, (for example, to individual learning centers), end with a standing challenge.
- If you are going to do another activity with them for which they need to be seated, add one more challenge to the above list.
- For instance, you might invite them to sit down if they are ready to have some fun.

The Four Seasons

Theme Connection
Seasons

Ready

- Use this fingerplay for any of the four seasons.
- This is a fun way for the children to come together at the beginning of their day.

Set

- Sit in a circle with the children, reciting the words below and teaching them the corresponding actions.

Go

- The actions appear in the parentheses next to each line. The words are as follows:

> *I like the world in autumn (winter; spring; summer).* (point toward self; circle arms for "world")
> *The days are oh so crisp (bright; new; long).* (rub hands together with delight)
> *This one season of the four* (hold up one finger on one hand & four on other)
> *Holds joys that can't be missed (for our delight; for me and you; that are so strong).* (cup hands to heart)
> *I find some joy in every day.* (hold hand above eyes, as though searching)
> *And I'll tell you the reason.* (point toward self and then toward teacher or other children)

There is no doubt about it, (wave pointer finger back and forth)
I'm glad there are four seasons! (applaud!)

Here We Go

Ready

- Use this activity when it is time to move from where the children have gathered to another part of the classroom.

Set

- Motor skills do not develop automatically from an immature to a mature level. They must be taught and practiced just like any other skill in early childhood.
- This activity offers an opportunity for the children to experience a variety of locomotor (traveling) skills.

Go

- Challenge the children to move to their next destination in one of the following ways, making sure to ask them only to perform skills within their capabilities:

  - jumping (two feet)
  - hopping (one foot)
  - marching
  - walking
  - galloping
  - skipping

Another Transition Idea

- Add the following descriptors to the above skills to provide varying movement elements and help the children have a more complete experience of the motor skills listed.
- When appropriate, invite the children to perform the skills in the following ways:

  - forward
  - backward
  - sideways

- in a straight line
- in a curving line
- in a zigzag path
- at a high level
- at a low level
- lightly
- strongly
- slowly
- quickly

Let's Solve a Problem

Ready

- As mentioned in the Introduction, the ability to solve problems in a variety of ways is essential to cognitive development and to simply growing up!
- It is important to allow children to demonstrate their responses to these challenges in their own way.
- You can still decide on parameters for behavior, but encourage creativity, not conformity.
- For example, when asked to move in a backward direction, some children will walk, others might jump, and still others might tiptoe.

Set

- Before using any of the following challenges, be sure the children understand that there is no one right way to respond.

Go

- Invite the children to transition to another area in the classroom or to another activity in the following ways:

  - using only one hand and one foot (or one hand and two feet; two hands and one foot)
  - like any four-legged animal
  - in a crooked (rounded; pointed) shape
  - as though walking on eggs, trying not to break them
  - using any locomotor skill but walking or running

Separate Ways

Ready

- Use this activity when the children are transitioning to free time or different learning centers.
- It will make the transition enjoyable and reassure those children who are experiencing separation anxiety.

Set

- Explain to the children that when they hear this song it is time to go to free time or individual learning centers.

Go

- Sing the following to the tune of "London Bridge."

> *Now we go our separate ways,*
> *Separate ways, separate ways.*
> *Now we go our separate ways*
> *We'll come back together soon!*

One Little, Two Little

Ready

- Use this activity when you want to dismiss a few children at a time from the group.
- This is helpful for avoiding chaos with a large group.
- This song is also an exercise in counting.

Set

- Before singing this song, explain that you will point to certain children when it is their turn to leave the circle.

Go

- Pointing to the appropriate number of children, sing the following words to the tune of "Ten Little Indians."

> *One little, two little, three little children*
> *Four little, five little, six little children*
> *Seven little, eight little, nine little children*
> *Leaving from our circle (or off to learning centers).*

Moving Like Animals

Ready

- Use this activity to encourage children to transition into their day by moving like different animals.
- Moving like an animal stimulates the imagination, allows an opportunity to practice a variety of movements, and helps create empathy for the world's creatures.

Set

- Dismiss one child at a time from the group with the following poem.
- Explain that you will point to one child and she is to name an animal and then move like that animal to free play or center time.

Go
- Let the fun begin!

> *Hello, (Rebecca)*
> *We're glad you're here today.*
> *Won't you choose an animal*
> *That you want to portray?* (child names an animal)
> *Well, (Rebecca's) chosen*
> *To be a (horse) today.*
> *Won't you show me how a (horse)*
> *Would move on this (Wednesday)?*

Animal Environments

Ready
- This activity offers children an opportunity to think about the world's creatures and their environments.

Set
- Talk with the children about different animals and where they live.

Go
- Choose an animal environment (for example, the jungle, the ocean, the forest, or the sky) and challenge the children to name animals that live in that environment.
- Invite them to leave the group as one of those animals.

Note: Repeat this activity often, sometimes using the same environment and sometimes a different one!

Pass a Sound

Ready

- This activity may seem like it's just for fun, but it also teaches sound discrimination. It is perfect if you're focusing on an animal theme.

Set

- Sit in a circle with the children.

Go

- Begin by making the sound of a familiar animal.
- In turn, each child imitates the sound as closely as possible, all the way around the circle.
- When the sound comes back to you, ask the children what animal makes that sound.
- The children shout out their responses and the game begins again with someone else initiating a sound.

Note: If time is short, allow two or three children to take a turn making an animal sound. Then, each time you play it, you can choose two or three others.

- Invite the children to leave the circle like one of the animals whose sound you imitated.

Cleanup

You can ensure that cleanup is a pleasant task for young children by making it an agreeable and a necessary routine, and you can help children learn responsibility.

Although experts vary in their suggestions regarding the length of notice to be given prior to cleanup time, they agree that it is important to give children warning of forthcoming shifts in activity. Isenberg and Jalongo (1997) suggest 10-, 5-, and 1-minute warnings to begin cleanup; Gordon and Browne (1996) suggest a 5-minute warning. Essa (1999) recommends one minute of warning for each year of the child's age (for example, four minutes for four-year-olds). Whatever amount of time you determine is appropriate, establish a signal, such as a flick of the lights, to indicate that it is time to begin wrapping up. A chant can be a signal that warning time has elapsed and that the actual cleanup must begin. This chapter contains chants you can use for this purpose.

Once cleanup starts, a number of possibilities can make it both quick and fun. Music is certainly valuable. Beaty (1984) suggests playing a favorite recording and challenging the children to finish before the song ends. Any lively song is fine as long as it is one with which the children are familiar so they can anticipate the ending. This chapter also offers lots of songs the children can sing themselves as they go about the task of cleaning up.

As with any aspect of early childhood, repetition is key. Initially, sing these songs yourself over a period of days as the children clean. They will soon become familiar enough to sing along with you and eventually to even sing them on their own.

Imagination can also make cleanup fun. Children love to pretend, and in this chapter you will find activities that give them that opportunity, as well. This chapter also offers activities that provide valuable experience with various elements of movement, including pathways, direction, force, and flow, and with such concepts as color, the alphabet, and counting.

You can use the activities on pages 36-42 ("It is Time to Clean Up" to "Zoom, Zoom") as signals to begin cleanup. Some serve both as signals and as a cleanup activity. The activities on pages 42-52 ("A-B-C Clean" to "Clean Up by Color") are intended for use during the cleaning up process.

It's Time to Clean Up

Ready

- This activity uses a chant as a signal that warning time has elapsed and actual cleanup must begin.

Set

- Be sure the children understand that, as soon as they hear this simple three-line chant, they must begin to clean up.

Go

- Use your most animated voice to say the following:

> *It's time to clean up.*
> *It's time to clean up.*
> *It's time to clean up right now!*

Ready-Set-Clean

Ready

- Children will enjoy this call-and-response cleanup signal.

Set

- Teach the children this brief call-and-response chant, explaining that it will serve as a final warning signal to begin cleanup.

Go

- After using the preliminary warning signals you have established for the countdown to cleanup, say the following:

> *Ready...Who's ready?*
> *[Children respond: "I am!"]*
>
> *Set...Who's set?*
> *[Children respond: "I am!"]*
>
> *Ready—set—clean!*

A Flick of the Lights

Ready

- This chant, along with the simple actions that accompany it, can help make children *glad* it is cleanup time!

Set

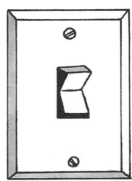

- Explain to the children that when they hear the following chant, they should stop what they are doing.
- Then they blink their eyes and clap their hands to turn themselves into "magic cleaning elves!"

Go

- Chant the following, accompanying the first two lines with a flick of the lights and a clap of the hands!

  A flick of the lights,
  A clap of my hands,
  Means cleanup time
  Throughout the land!

Another Transition Idea

- Wave a "magic wand" or sprinkle "magic dust" to turn the children into cleaning elves.

Freeze, Shake, & Clean

Ready

- Children love to move and they love to be silly.
- This final alert that it is time to clean up offers them an opportunity to do both.
- It is also a great exercise in body-part identification, an important first step in movement education, and it is a science concept, as well.

Set

- Let the children know what to do when they hear you call out the following instructions.

Go

- Once you have given the children their initial warning signals, call out "Freeze!"
- The children freeze wherever they are.
- Unfreeze one body part at a time by calling out its name. (For example, when you say "hands," the children relax their hands.)
- Once the children are completely unfrozen, call out "Shake!"
- The children shake out their body parts.
- Finally, call out "Clean!"

A Special Breath

Ready

- Deep breathing promotes relaxation and self-control.
- It is also a good way to help children pause and ready themselves for whatever comes next.
- Use a special breath, either as a preliminary or final signal for cleanup.

Set

- Teach the children what you mean by a "special breath," explaining that you are using it as a cue that it is cleanup time.

Go

- Call out "It is time for a special breath."
- The children stop what they are doing, bend low, and breathe in slowly through their noses, rising as they do.
- Once they have inhaled completely, they gradually let their breath out through their mouths, slowly collapsing their upper torsos.
- Do this only twice so the children don't hyperventilate.
- The children are now ready to clean!

Hi-Ho

Ready

- When the children hear you begin to sing the following little song, they know it is time to stop, look, listen, and then clean!

Set

- The words make cleaning sound like fun and incorporate the concepts of *up, down, high,* and *low.*

Go

- Sing the following to the tune of "It's Off to Work We Go."

> *Hi-ho, hi-ho*
> *It's off to clean we go.*
> *We'll clean up high*
> *And clean down low,*
> *Hi-ho, hi-ho!*

Another Transition Idea

- An alternative is to have the children repeat the song, incorporating the following actions (in parentheses), before they begin to clean.

> *Hi-ho, hi-ho* (pump fist into air twice)
> *It's off to clean we go.* (mime sweeping)
> *We'll clean up high* (reach high)
> *And clean down low* (bend low)
> *Hi-ho, hi-ho!* (again pump fist into air twice)

Let's Clean the Room

Ready

- Use this song as a warning signal or as a song for the children to sing as they clean.

Set

- Because it is short and sung to a familiar melody the children will learn it in no time.

Go

- Sing the following to the tune of "Pop Goes the Weasel."

> *It's time to put our things away.*
> *It's time to clean the room.*
> *It's important to be neat.*
> *Let's clean the room!*

1-2-3-Clean

Ready

- This can be both a final signal and an activity to use for cleanup.
- It also offers experience with counting and a bit of rhythm.

Set

- Let the children know what to expect and what is expected of them!

Go

- Follow your preliminary signals for cleanup with a loudly spoken "1-2-3-clean," accompanied by four hand claps or four taps on a drum.
- When the children hear this signal, they know they are supposed to *count* each item they pick up and put away!

Countdown to Cleanup

Ready

- This is another activity involving numbers, this time counting backward!

Set

- Talk to the children about counting down.
- Ask them:

    Have you ever heard a countdown prior to a shuttle launch?

    What do you say after the counting reaches zero?

    (After *zero*, the words *blast off* are called out.)

- Then explain this activity to them.

Go

- As a final warning signal that it is time to begin cleanup, count backward from 10 to 0 with as much drama as possible; substitute the words *clean up* for *blast off.*
- As the children begin to clean up, start the countdown again *at a much slower pace*, the idea being that the children will finish cleanup by the time you reach zero.

Note: You may want to begin counting down from a higher number.

- End by saying, "All clean."

Zoom, Zoom

Ready

- This song is fast paced and fun.
- Use it as a final warning signal.

Set

- Use this song as a final warning signal; the children can sing it as they clean.

Go

- Teach the children this song, sung to the tune of "Hail, Hail, the Gang's All Here."

> *Zoom, zoom*
> *Let's clean the room.*
> *It's time for us to move on,*
> *So let's get a move on.*
> *Zoom, zoom*
> *Let's clean the room.*
> *Let's clean up the room right now!*

A-B-C Clean

Ready

- This cleanup activity provides practice with letter recognition!
- It will be helpful to have the alphabet posted where all the children can see it.

Set

- Explain the rules of this clean-up game. Tell the children that you will point to a letter and ask them to pick up only items beginning with that letter.

Go

- Point to a letter on a posted alphabet.
- Ask the children to pick up only items beginning with that letter.
- Even if there are no items for a certain letter, point to it anyway and let the *children* determine whether or not there is an appropriate item.

Note: If the children are not sufficiently familiar with the alphabet, you may want to assign the letters in order, or say the letter as you point to it. Or, ask the children to pick up items that rhyme with a certain word. For example, ask them to pick up items that rhyme with the word "sock."

Another Transition Idea

- When the children know and can recognize letters, adapt this cleanup game so they pick up items on their own, saying aloud, "This begins with the letter...."

I Spy

Ready

- This activity is a take-off on the old guessing game, "I Spy."
- Guessing is a form of problem solving, an essential cognitive skill.

Set

- Sit in a circle with the children.

Go

- Say to each child in turn, "I spy with my little eye something that begins with the letter...."
- That child guesses what the item might be (it is always best if there is more than one possible "correct" answer) and then gets up to clean or put it away.

Note: If you feel it is too much pressure for just one child to guess an item, modify the game so all the children can guess, but the child whose turn it is does the cleaning.

Another Transition Idea

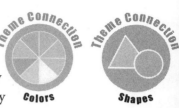

Colors   Shapes

- Modify this activity by saying either: "I spy with my little eye something in the color..." or "I spy with my little eye something in a _____ shape."

Cleanup Imagery

Ready

- Using imagination contributes to self-expression and problem solving.
- Let the children respond to each of the following images any way they see fit!

Set

- Talk with the children about the images below, discussing the movements involved in each.

Go

- Ask the children to clean up while pretending to be:

  - Vacuum cleaners
  - Elves
  - Garbage trucks
  - Giant cranes

Another Transition Idea

- To incorporate the theme of occupations, ask the children to clean up while pretending to be:

    - Construction workers
    - Homemakers
    - Custodians

The Path to Cleanliness

Ready

- *Space* is one element of movement.
- When moving through general or shared space, there are pathways and directions.
- Pathways can be straight, curving, zigzag, forward, sideways, or backward.

Set

- Before asking children to move in the different pathways and directions while cleaning up, familiarize them with these concepts and give them a chance to explore them.

Go

- When it is time to clean up, challenge the children to move only in the ways you indicate as they pick things up and put them where they belong.
- Invite them to clean while using straight, curving, or zigzagging pathways, or while moving forward, backward, or sideways!

Tiptoe to Tiptop Shape

Before

- Muscle tension, a movement element, determines how lightly or strongly a movement is performed.
- Control over muscle tension is essential to the ability to relax.

Set

- Talk to the children about moving *lightly*.
- Can they think of an animal that moves lightly and quietly?
- Ask them to demonstrate.
- How does a robot move? Lightly or heavily?
- Invite them to show you.

Go

- Challenge the children to clean up while moving as lightly and quietly as possible. Or ask them to pretend to be one of the animals mentioned during your discussion—as long as it is one that moves lightly and quietly!
- After a while, or next time, invite them to clean up as though they were robots so they can experience the contrast in muscle tension.

The Cleaning Machine

Before

- Cleaning can be "cool" when you use the right imagery!
- Children are fascinated by machines and how they work.

Set

- Talk to the children about machines that perform tasks for us that people once had to do by hand, such as washing machines or dishwashers.
- Do the children think that someday there might be machines that do even *more* work for us?
- What kind of work?
- What do they think those machine might look like?

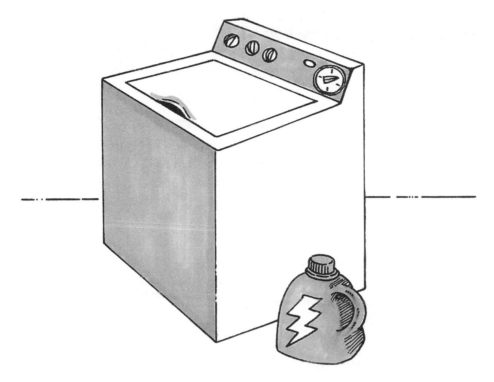

Go

- Invite the children to imagine they are cleaning machines, any kind they want to be, as they go about the work of picking up and putting away.
- They can recite the following chant as they work:

> *I'm a lean, mean*
> *Cleaning machine.*
> *When I'm finished here*
> *This place will be clean!*

Once Upon a Time

Ready

- Children love stories, and they love to pretend to *be* the characters in the stories they hear.
- This clean-up activity offers them both!

Set

- Sit with the children and tell them a story about a child named Tracy, who *loved* to help clean the house.

Tracy's parents appreciated all the things Tracy did around the house. For example, Tracy made the bed every morning, removed the clean dishes from the dishwasher after school, and set the table for dinner every evening. Tracy also enjoyed vacuuming and dusting because it seemed like a dance! But Tracy's favorite chore was picking up toys and putting them away because she liked things to look neat. When Tracy went to bed at night, there was such a feeling of satisfaction. Not only did Tracy's parents have less to do, but Tracy felt a sense of pride that made for a very good night's sleep!

- If you like, briefly discuss the children's reactions to the story. Do they do any of the chores mentioned?

Go

- Ask the children to imagine themselves as Tracy as they clean up!

Singing While We Work

Ready

- There is nothing like a song to turn an ordinary task into a pleasant one.

Set

- The children can sing this little ditty as they go about the work of cleaning up.

Go

- Sing the following to the tune of "Whistle While You Work."

  Singing while we work,
  We're happy to be neat.
  We pick up here and pick up there
  Until our job's complete.

- Sing the song over and over until the task of cleaning up is complete.

Time to Clean I

Ready
- Talk to the children about the importance of taking pride in one's work and environment.

Set
- Talk with the children about the meaning of the phrase *spick and span.*

Go
- Sing the following to the tune of "Row, Row, Row Your Boat."

> *Time, time, time to clean*
> *Time to clean our space.*
> *We will get it spick and span*
> *Because it is our place!*

Time to Clean II

Ready
- Discuss the concept of taking pride in a job well done.

Set
- The children sing this song as they clean.

Go
- Sing the following to the tune of "Jingle Bells."

> *Time to clean,*
> *Time to clean,*
> *Time to clean up now.*
> *We will do the best darn job,*
> *And then we'll take a bow!*

- When cleanup is done, have the children take a bow!

Happy to Be Clean

Ready

- Talk to the children about pride and joy. Ask them:

    What do you think those words mean?

    When have you felt those emotions?

    Why would cleaning up make you feel pride and joy?

Set

- The children can sing this song as they go about the job of cleaning up.

Go

- Sing the following to the tune of "Old MacDonald."

    We are happy to be clean
    To make our space real neat.
    We will work with pride and joy
    Until our job's complete.
    We will pick up here
    And pick up there.
    Here we clean, there we clean
    Everywhere we keep clean.
    We are happy to be clean
    To make our space real neat!

Celebrate Cleaning!

Theme Connection — Seasons

Theme Connection — Holidays & Celebrations

Ready

- Get the children thinking with this activity, which also has thematic connections!

Set

- Talk about the season or upcoming holiday with the children *before* it is time to clean.

Go

● Challenge the children to pretend to be something related to the season, or an upcoming holiday, as they clean.

● For example, they might pretend to be Santa or a snowperson in winter, Cupid in February, or a ghost in October.

Clean Up by Color

Ready

● This activity works on color recognition as it makes cleanup fun. Color is both an art and a science concept.

Set

● If you think it will be helpful, post a color chart where the children can see it.

Go

● Challenge the children to pick up everything blue (or red, green, yellow, etc.) and to place it where it belongs.

● What colors are left?

● As the children work, they can sing the following to the tune of "I'm a Little Teapot."

> *I put away the [blue] things*
> *Watch and see.*
> *I know my colors.*
> *Aren't you proud of me?*

Another Transition Idea

Shapes

- Play this game with shapes, an art and math concept. For example, ask the children to pick up and put away everything that is round, square, wide, triangular, pointed, and so on. What shapes are left?

Snacks and Lunch

If you teach in an all-day program, you most likely have three transitions involving food: a morning snack, lunch, and an afternoon snack. If the children arrive early enough, you may serve them breakfast, making a grand total of *four* transitions involving food. In any case, you will need lots of food-related activities to keep these transitions calm and meaningful.

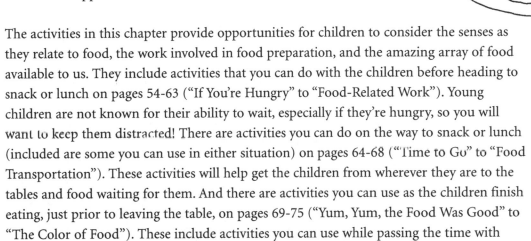

Of course, any activities related to food concepts are learning experiences. Nutrition is an important science concept, which means that you can also use the activities in this section for *any* transition when your weekly or monthly theme is nutrition. There is much to be learned and appreciated about food in all its forms.

The activities in this chapter provide opportunities for children to consider the senses as they relate to food, the work involved in food preparation, and the amazing array of food available to us. They include activities that you can do with the children before heading to snack or lunch on pages 54-63 ("If You're Hungry" to "Food-Related Work"). Young children are not known for their ability to wait, especially if they're hungry, so you will want to keep them distracted! There are activities you can do on the way to snack or lunch (included are some you can use in either situation) on pages 64-68 ("Time to Go" to "Food Transportation"). These activities will help get the children from wherever they are to the tables and food waiting for them. And there are activities you can use as the children finish eating, just prior to leaving the table, on pages 69-75 ("Yum, Yum, the Food Was Good" to "The Color of Food"). These include activities you can use while passing the time with those children who are finished eating and are waiting for their classmates to finish.

As with the activities in the other chapters of *Teachable Transitions*, those found here will also give children a chance to sing, chant, interact, solve problems, exercise their imaginations, use language, and experience a variety of movements and movement elements. The transitions for snacks and lunch are every bit as enjoyable as the actual eating!

If You're Hungry

Ready

- This fingerplay will help the children work up an appetite and an appreciation for the food.
- Because it is similar to a song that the children probably know, it will not take them long to join in.

Set

- Sit in a circle with the children.

Go

- Sing and perform the following to the tune of "If You're Happy and You Know It."
- The actions appear in parentheses following each line.

If you're hungry and you know it, lick your lips. (lick lips)
If you're hungry and you know it, lick your lips. (lick lips)
If you're hungry and you know it,
Then your face will surely show it. (look hungry)
If you're hungry and you know it, lick your lips. (lick lips)

If you're hungry and you know it, rub your tummy.
   (rub tummy.)
If you're hungry and you know it, rub your tummy.
   (rub tummy.)
If you're hungry and it's time to eat,
Then let's get up and on our feet. (stand)
If you're hungry and you know it, rub your tummy. (rub
   tummy while standing)

My Tummy's Getting Hungry

Ready

- This activity is another fingerplay you can use just before heading to snack time or lunch.
- Most children will find the concept of a growling tummy quite hilarious.

Set

- Sit in a circle with the children, and ask them if they have ever heard their tummies "growl" when hungry.

Go

- Sing and perform the following to the tune of "I'm a Little Teapot."

My tummy's getting hungry
(rub tummy)
Hear it growl. (place hand at ear)
It needs some food to fill it up now. (pantomime using a utensil to bring food to mouth)
My tummy must be empty (look at tummy)
As it can be.
Yes! It must be time to eat! (raise pointer finger toward ceiling on "yes," then point first at wrist, where a watch would be, and finally at open mouth)

Hey, Hey, It's Time to Eat

Ready

- This is a fun, quick song you and the children can sing together just before heading to snack or lunch.
- Or use it as a signal to alert children to the fact that it is time for lunch or snack and they should finish whatever they are doing.

Set

- Sing with enthusiasm!

Go

- Sing the following to the tune of "Hail, Hail, the Gang's All Here."

> *Hey, hey*
> *It's time to eat.*
> *We're so glad it's lunch (snack) time.*
> *We're so glad it's lunch (snack) time.*
> *Hey, hey*
> *It's time to eat.*
> *Let's not wait a minute more!*

This Is the Way We...

Ready

- This activity offers children a chance to use their imaginations and move, as they also consider the variety of tasks involved in preparing and eating meals.

Set

- Talk with the children about the actions involved in the song below.
- How many of them help with some of these chores at home?

Go

- Sing the following to the tune of "Here We Go 'Round the Mulberry Bush." Invite the children to act out the verses.

> *This is the way we set the table,*
> *Set the table, set the table.*
> *This is the way we set the table*
> *Here at (name of school or center).*

- Additional verses:
  > *Second verse: Serve the food*
  > *Third verse: Eat our food*
  > *Fourth verse: Clear the table*
  > *Fifth verse: Wash the dishes*

Being Food

Ready

- Children love to pretend, and this imagination-invoking activity gives them that opportunity!
- Remember that self-expression, not conformity, is the goal.
- Encourage self-expression by pointing out the variety of responses.

Set

- Before you begin, talk to the children about the images listed below.
- Are they familiar with the images?

Go

- Challenge the children to show you what they would look like if they were the following:

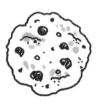

  - soup sloshing in a bowl
  - a sandwich
  - a cookie
  - an egg
  - a piece of celery
  - a carrot stick
  - an orange
  - a potato

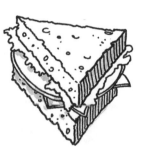

Before and After Food

Ready

- Children may not give any thought to the origin of some foods.
- This activity will give them an opportunity to consider the "before and after" of food.

Set

- Talk with the children about the following list. Talk about what each of these items looks like and how the pairs go from one to the other.

Go

- Challenge the children to demonstrate what the following foods look like:

    - an apple hanging on a tree/applesauce
    - an egg/scrambled eggs
    - a carrot/carrot juice
    - a piece of bread going into the toaster/a piece of toast coming out

Get Ready, Spaghetti

Ready

- This activity is similar to the previous activity as it encourages children to consider the before and after of certain food.
- It also serves as a relaxation exercise (contracting and releasing the muscles) as the children wait for snack or lunch.

Set

- Talk to the children about the differences between uncooked and cooked spaghetti, letting them come up with ideas on their own.
- If they need prompting, you can ask them to tell you which is straighter, and which is firmer.

Go

- Invite the children to demonstrate with their bodies uncooked and cooked spaghetti.
- Alternate between the two, ending with the cooked version so the children's muscles are relaxed.

My Favorite Food

Ready

- This activity encourages children to reflect and to use language.

Set

- Explain that one child will tell the rest of the group what his favorite food is and why.
- Then everyone will take on the shape of that food.

Go

- One child tells the rest of the group what her favorite food is and why.
- Everyone takes on the shape of that food. The process continues with the next child until everyone has had a turn.

Another Transition Idea

- Instead of asking the children to tell you their favorite foods, ask each child to name a food or drink related to the *season*.
- For example, they might say a pumpkin or an apple for fall, an ear of corn for summer, or hot cocoa for winter.

Theme Connection
Seasons

Alphabet Soup

Ready

- This is a great activity for getting children to think and learn about the alphabet.
- The last part of the activity helps them think about the straight and curving lines that make up the letters, using both mind and body.

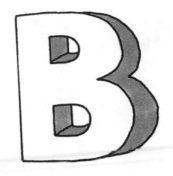

Set

- Post the alphabet, written in large letters, where all the children can see it.

Go

- Point to a letter and ask the children to think of as many foods beginning with that letter as they can.
- When they can't think of any more, ask them to make the shape of the letter with their bodies.
- Move to another letter.

Note: To help the children experience success, begin with letters that have the fewest lines, such as C, T, I, X, and O.

Food-Related Machines

Ready

- A number of household machines are related to food and beverages.
- Children will love the opportunity to pretend to *be* these machines.

Set

- Talk to the children about each of the items in the following list. Ask the children:

  - Have you ever seen these machines?
  - What do they look like?
  - How do they work?

Go

- Challenge the children to show you what they would look like if they were one of the following food-related machines, or *in* one of them.

  - can opener (electric or hand-held)
  - coffee maker (drip or percolator)
  - dishwasher
  - cake mixer (electric or hand-held)
  - blender or food processor

Food Forms

Ready

- This activity requires lots of imagination and will result in any number of interpretations, and that is just what you want!
- Divergent problem solving is necessary for both creative and critical thinking skills.

Set

- However you choose to use this activity, you will first want to discuss the images with the children.

Go

- Ask the children to demonstrate the following food forms:

  - mashed
  - frozen
  - overcooked/mushy
  - lumpy
  - melting
  - thick
  - bubbling
  - sticky

Another Transition Idea

- Once the children are familiar with this imagery, challenge them to demonstrate these food forms while moving to snack or lunch.

What Food Am I?

Ready

- Do this activity with the children as they wait for the food or tables to be ready.
- Cognitive skills are promoted as the children engage in guessing. And, because the activity is cooperative in nature, social skills are also enhanced.

Set

- Sit in a circle with the children and explain that one child will form the shape or action of a food and the other children will guess what food he is.

Go

- One child goes to the center of the circle and takes on the shape (or action) of a familiar food.
- For example, a child might demonstrate a curved shape for a banana.
- The rest of the children try to guess what it is.
- Once they have guessed, all of the children take on the same shape or perform the same action before the game continues with a different child who moves into the center of the circle.

Food-Related Work

Ready

- This activity will give children an appreciation for food-related jobs.

Set

- Talk about the roles of the people listed below. Ask the children:
  - What do the people in these jobs do?
  - How do these jobs relate to food?

Go

- Ask the children to demonstrate actions that might be performed by people in these food-related occupations:

  - chef
  - baker
  - truck driver
  - grocery store clerk
  - waiter or waitress
  - restaurant host or hostess

Time to Go

Ready
- This activity will help children wait for snack or lunchtime.

Set
- Sing this song with the children on the way to snack or lunch, or sing it beforehand.

Go
- Sing to the tune of "Eensy Weensy Spider."

> *It's time to go to snack (lunch) now.*
> *It's time for us to eat.*
> *We hope that you are ready*
> *To serve us up a treat.*
>
> *It's time to go to snack (lunch) now,*
> *And we can hardly wait.*
> *To see what kind of tasty food*
> *You've placed upon our plates.*

We're Heading to Lunch Now

Ready
- Use this activity as the children make the transition to the table.

Set
- Use this song to announce that it is lunch or snack time, or while children are walking to the tables.

Go
- Teach the children these four lines, sung to the tune of "On Top of Old Smokey."

> *We're heading to lunch (snack) now*
> *Where we get to eat.*
> *We're glad 'cause we're hungry*
> *And eating's a treat!*

We Are Hungry

Ready

● This activity involves a familiar song.

Set

● Teach the children this song so they can announce their imminent arrival at the table.

Go

● Sing the following to the tune of "Where Is Thumbkin?"

> *We are hungry.*
> *We are hungry.*
> *Here we come.*
> *Here we come.*
> *It's time for us to eat.*
> *We're hoping for a treat.*
> *Here we are.*
> *Here we are.*

Popcorn

Ready

● This activity gives children an opportunity to practice the locomotor skill of jumping (or hopping) and to experience the movement element of force.

Set

● Talk to the children about popcorn. Ask them:
  How do popcorn kernels start small and then get larger as they are heated?
  Is popcorn light or heavy?

Go

- Ask the children to imagine they are tiny little popcorn kernels on the floor, pretending that the floor is a stove or microwave.
- As the heat gets to them, they can begin to pop.
- Finally, invite them to move to snack or lunch like popcorn popping!

Food in Motion

Ready

- This activity offers another opportunity to pretend!
- As they pretend, children are solving problems creatively and experiencing a variety of movements.

Set

- Discuss the following images with the children before asking them to experience them.
- Ask the children, "How would you describe ...?"

Go

- Challenge the children to move like the following:

  - a grape rolling across a table
  - milk being poured
  - pancake batter being poured
  - bacon sizzling in the pan
  - spaghetti right out of the box

Food-Related Motion

Ready

- This activity is similar to the previous one.
- However, instead of pretending to be different kinds of food, the children will move in ways *related* to food.

Set

- Spend as much time as necessary discussing the following images with the children, particularly the ones that might be new to them, such as molasses or stomping grapes.

Go

- Challenge the children to move to snack or lunch in the following ways:

  - like the odor of food floating through the air
  - as though moving through peanut butter or marshmallow fluff
  - as slowly as molasses being poured
  - like a fizzy drink
  - like a liquid boiling
  - as though in a blender
  - as though walking through mashed potatoes
  - as though stomping grapes
  - as though walking on eggs they don't want to break

The Shape of Food

Theme Connection

Shapes

Ready

- This activity offers children a fun way to move to snack or lunch *and* an opportunity to experience the movement element of shapes, which is both an art and a math concept.

Set

- Before beginning, discuss the shapes of the following food with the children, remembering that some of them (for example, a cookie) can have more than one possibility.

Go

- Ask the children to move to snack or lunch in the shape of the following:

  - a cookie
  - a carrot stick
  - an egg
  - a piece of broccoli
  - a watermelon
  - a banana
  - a slice of cheese
  - a Popsicle or lollipop

Food Transportation

Ready

- Use this activity to move the children from wherever they are to the tables where their food is waiting *and* to promote consideration of transportation, which is a social studies concept.

Set

- Talk to the children about the fact that not all foods are grown or are available in all areas.
- Grapefruit and oranges, for example, are grown in a tropical climate such as Florida. If people who live in the middle of the country want to have grapefruits and oranges, the fruit has to be transported from one place to another.
- Discuss the various modes of transportation, listed below, which bring food from one area to another.

Go

- Challenge the children to move like the following forms of transportation:

  - a truck
  - a boat
  - an airplane
  - a train

Another Transition Idea

- Individuals also use different forms of transportation to move food from one place to another.
- Ask the children to move like the following:

  - a grocery cart
  - a car
  - a bicycle

- Can the children think of any others?

Yum, Yum, the Food Was Good

Ready

- This activity is especially fun if children have sung "Hey, Hey, It's Time to Eat" (see page 55) on their way to snack or lunch.
- It also instills gratitude into the eating experience.

Set

- Talk to the children about gratitude.

Go

- Sing the following to the tune of "Hail, Hail, the Gang's All Here."

> Yum, yum
> The food is gone.
> We have finished eating.
> We have finished eating.
> Yum, yum
> The food is gone.
> We are grateful for the food!

That Was Yummy

Ready

- This activity uses another enjoyable song that demonstrates appreciation, while also focusing on three body parts.

Set

- Tell the children that when they hear the name of a body part they should point to it.

Go

- Sing the following to the tune of "This Old Man."

    That was good.
    That was yummy.
    That was good food
    In my tummy.
    I'm so glad for food to eat
    I feel good from head to feet!

Thank You

Ready

- We can never teach children too much about gratitude and appreciation.

Set

- This activity gives them an opportunity to thank the teachers or cafeteria workers who brought them their food.

Go

- Sing the following to the tune of "I'm a Little Teapot."

  We thank you for the good food
  We just ate.
  We want you to know
  We appreciate
  All of the nice things that you do.
  So, we just want to say
  Thank you!

Another Transition Idea

- To turn this song into a fingerplay, add the actions that appear in brackets next to each line of the lyrics.

  We thank you for the good food (point at self and then person(s) being thanked)
  We just ate. (mime eating with fork)
  We want you to know (same as for line 1)
  We appreciate (put hand to heart)
  All of the nice things that you do (hold up one finger at a time, as though counting)
  So, we just want to say (hands at either side of mouth, as though calling out to someone)
  Thank you! (blow kiss)

What I Liked Best

Ready

- This activity allows children to reflect and use language while also demonstrating appreciation.

Set

- Explain to the children that as they finish eating, you will ask them what they enjoyed most about what they ate.

Go

- As each child finishes eating, ask her to tell what she enjoyed most about what she just ate.

2-4-6-8

Ready

- This age-old cheer is a fun call-and-response activity for demonstrating gratitude.

Set

- Teach the children how this activity works, explaining that once they have heard you call out your two lines, they should respond appropriately, with "the cooks," "the teachers," or whoever else might have been responsible for preparing and serving the food.
- If possible, use the names of individuals.

Go

- Simply call out:

  2-4-6-8
  Who do we appreciate?

- The children then offer the appropriate response.

Fill in the Blanks

Ready

- This fill-in-the-blank activity gives children another opportunity to use language.

Set

- Explain how the activity works and reassure the children that, although there will be repeats among the food items, they can also use their own descriptions.

Go

- As each child finishes eating, he chooses one food he ate and one word to describe it, filling in the blanks as follows: "I ate a _____, and it was _____."
- An example would be: "I ate a piece of pizza, and it was cheesy."

I Spy

Ready

- Children riding in cars have played this activity for decades. It provides an opportunity for children to consider the letters of the alphabet and to do some reflecting.

Set

- Explain the rules, telling children that for this version of the game they can only spy something on the table or that is related to food and within sight of the table.

Go

- Simply chant:

    I spy
    With my little eye
    Something that begins with...

- Add a letter at the end, making sure it is a letter that begins a word the children can guess fairly easily.

Note: For children who are not yet familiar with letters, say, "Something that rhymes with..."

Stand Up/Sit Down

Ready

- Play this active game with children who have finished eating.
- This activity was introduced in the Arrival chapter and has been modified here for use during snack or lunchtime.

Set

- Explain to the children that they are to listen to each of the statements you make and take the appropriate action if the statement applies to them.

Go

- Invite the children to alternately stand up or remain seated if they:

  - cleaned their plate
  - have eaten any of those foods before
  - ate something new today
  - ate something green (red, orange, etc.)
  - ate something crunchy (smooth, chewy, etc.)
  - ate something salty (sweet, tart)
  - ate something hot (cold, warm)
  - thought the food was great!

The Color of Food

Colors   Shapes

Ready

- Food, color, and shape are often related to one another.
- This activity offers children the opportunity to consider all three.

Set

- Ask the children to name all the foods they can think of that are red, orange, yellow, green, or purple.

Go

- Give the children one of the colors previously mentioned and challenge them to take on the shape of a food in that color.
- The other children guess what foods they are depicting.
- Repeat with other colors as time permits.

Outside the Classroom

This chapter covers transitions that involve, among others, going outdoors for play time or recess; leaving for field trips; or simply going to another area in the building. You will find activities that prepare children to leave the room, go out the door, down the hall, and outside. You will also find suggestions for times when the transition needs to be especially quiet, as when the children are going down a hallway past other classrooms.

Although *Teachable Transitions* can't possibly cover all the themes you may use as part of your curriculum, several of the activities address popular early childhood themes and may spark your own ideas for incorporating these themes and others into your transitions.

You will also want to let your imagination flow if your class is going on or coming from a field trip. Make those transitions more relevant by relating them in some way to the trip. For instance, if you went to a fire station, ask the children to move like water flowing through a hose or the hose being unwound from the truck and stretched out. Can they create a single hose with their bodies? If you went to a bakery, challenge the children to move in the shape of a rolling pin or a loaf of bread.

Sometimes transitions to outside the classroom involve arranging the children in single-file lines. When this is the case, make sure different children get to go first. Use a variety of methods to ensure this: on one day arrange the children alphabetically by first name; the next day use last names; on another day, ask all the children wearing green to line up first; on another day, line up by month of birth; and so on. This helps ensure fairness and gets the children's brain cells working!

As in the other chapters, this one also offers the children lots of opportunity to express themselves, use their imaginations, solve problems, sing, move, and have fun!

The activities on pages 78-89 ("Who's Ready to Go?" to "Chugga-Chugga") alert the children to the fact that it is time to leave the classroom and help get them to the door! Activities for moving from the classroom are on pages 89-98 ("We're Going Out the Door" to "What's the Weather?").

Who's Ready to Go?

Ready

- This call-and-response activity makes getting in line fun!

Set

- Teach the children their responses, explaining that at the end of the activity they're to form an orderly line at the door.

Go

- Use the following call-and-responses or make up your own.

> Teacher: *Who's ready to go?*
> Children: *We're ready to go!*
> Teacher: *Are you sure you're ready to go?*
> Children: *We're sure we're ready to go!*
> Teacher: *Show me you're ready to go!*
> Children: *We'll show you that now we're ready to go!*

- And they will!

1-2-3

Ready

- Use this activity as a signal that it is transition time and that you want the children to form an orderly line at the door.

Set

- Talk with the children about straight spines and good posture.
- Then explain what you will be expecting when you recite the following chant.

Go

- Dim the lights or use another signal to alert the children to an impending transition.
- Then call out the following:

1-2-3,
Look at me.
Show me a line
That's straight and fine!
1-2-3,
It's time to leave.
You should be waiting in line
With a nice straight spine!

Line Leader

Ready

- If you assign daily or weekly line leaders, use this little song to alert the leader that it is time to go to the door.

Set

- Let the line leader know that this song is his cue to go to the door!

Go

- Sing the following to the tune of "Oh Where, Oh Where, Can My Little Dog Be?"

    Oh where
    Oh where
    Can my line leader be?
    Oh where
    Oh where
    Can she (he) be?

Another Transition Idea

- If you are going to be the line leader, go to the door and sing the following to the tune of "The Farmer in the Dell."
- Let the children know that you expect them to join you!

    I'm standing here in line.
    I'm standing here in line.
    Hi-ho, the derry-o,
    I'm standing here in line.

Toward the Door

Ready

- Use imagery to stimulate children's imaginations and to get them to the door quietly!

Set

- Discuss the images before using them with the children.

Go

- Choose from among the following images or make up your own!
- Challenge the children to move toward the door as if they were:

  - a butterfly fluttering
  - an eagle soaring
  - a cat sneaking up on a bird
  - a weightless astronaut

Another Transition Idea

- If you are exploring the theme of the sea with the children, challenge them to move like any of the following (select one that they know):

  - a jellyfish
  - an eel
  - a starfish
  - the smallest fish in the ocean

Theme Connection

The Sea

What's My Line?

Ready

- This is a problem-solving activity for getting children into a line.

Set

- This may not work smoothly the first time, but as with much else in early childhood, repetition is the key!

Go

- Challenge the children to solve this problem: line up so every tummy but one is facing somebody else's back!

The Long & Short of It

Ready

- Use this problem-solving activity when you have plenty of time and you don't mind a little noise and confusion!
- It is an excellent exercise in the math concepts of quantity and length, so it is well worth the effort!

Set

- Use manipulatives to demonstrate how a series of items can be lined up from shortest to longest.

Go

- Challenge the children to form a line at the door that goes from the shortest to the tallest child. Another time, ask them to do the reverse—from tallest to shortest child.

What's My Shape?

Theme Connection

Shapes

Ready

- *Shape* is both an art and a math concept. It is also an element of movement, so it is definitely worth exploring with children.

Set

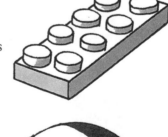

- Point out items of various shapes in the classroom.
- If necessary, offer children experience with the following shapes before using them for transition time.

Go

- Challenge the children to form a line and to stand in one of the following shapes:

  - round
  - narrow
  - pointed
  - crooked
  - "funny"

The Playground's Waiting

Ready

- This activity is appropriate if you are leaving the classroom to go outside to play.
- It is sure to put children in the mood!

Set

- Start to sing this song as a cue to the children to get ready to go outside, and they can join in as they get ready to go.

Go

- Sing the following to the tune of "She'll Be Comin' 'Round the Mountain."

> *Oh, the playground is waiting for us.*
> *Yes, the playground is waiting for us.*
> *Oh, the playground is waiting.*
> *Yes, the playground is waiting.*
> *Oh, the playground is waiting for us.*

Climb & Jump & Run Around

Ready

- Use this activity to alert children that it is time to get ready to go out to play.
- The emphasis is on being physically active once on the playground, an extremely important issue in today's society, with children leading more sedentary lifestyles and childhood obesity increasing at an alarming rate.

Set

● Whenever possible, talk with the children about how good it feels to *move*!

Go

● Sing the following to the tune of "Yankee Doodle."

> It is time to go outside.
> It's time for us to play.
> Climb and jump and run around
> On this beautiful day.
>
> Climb and jump and run around.
> We will have such fun.
> Leap and hop on the playground
> Until recess is done!

Another Transition Idea

● Sit in a circle with the children.
● Chant or sing this as a fingerplay.
● The words are repeated below, with suggested actions following them in brackets.

> It is time to go outside. (point to wrist and then to outside)
> It's time for us to play. (point to wrist, then spread fingers wide, palms facing out, hands crossing at the midline and then outward)
> Climb and jump and run around (pantomime climbing; jump hands upward, fingers spread; pantomime running with pointer and middle finger)
> On this beautiful day. (spread arms wide, palms up, crossing at the midline and moving outward)
>
> Climb and jump and run around. (repeat above actions for this line)
> We will have such fun. (draw imaginary smile with pointer finger, in the space in front of the mouth)
> Leap and hop on the playground (make "bounding" movements with hand in front of the body)
> Until recess is done! (point twice to the wrist, once again indicating time)

And Another Transition Idea

- If the children are going to the gym for physical education, use the following lyrics instead:

> *It is time to go to the gym.*
> *It's time for us to move.*
> *Run and jump and learn new skills*
> *So our health will improve!*

Goin' on a Field Trip

Ready

- If you are preparing for a field trip, this fingerplay can set the tone.
- It involves an action that crosses the midline, which is important for getting the left and right sides of the brain to "talk" to one another!

Set

- Sit in a circle with the children and discuss the nature of the upcoming field trip before teaching them the following fingerplay.
- Talk about the concept of learning as a way of being "all they can be."

Go

- The actions for the fingerplay follow each line.

> *We're goin' on a field trip* (walk pointer and
>   middle fingers)
> *To see what we can see.* (place hand above eyes)
> *There's so much that we can learn* (point twice to temple)
> *To be all that we can be!* (spread arms wide and then
>   cross, pressed to chest)

Another Transition Idea

- Use these words, with or without the arm movements, as a chant as you are leaving the room or building, riding on the bus, and so on.

Take My Hand

Ready

- This activity, a simple chant, is good to use if the children have been at learning centers and you want to gather them together to leave the room.

Set

- Move from center to center, inviting each child to join you as you chant the words below.

Go

- After chanting these three little lines to the children individually, lead them with a spirit of adventure toward the door.

Take my hand,
Come take my hand.
We're going on a journey!

Chugga-Chugga

Ready

- Use this activity both for preparing children to leave *and* for heading out the door to your destination.
- Children are fascinated with trains, and they love to pretend. This activity offers them an opportunity to pretend to be a train!

Set

- Before beginning, explain that one child at a time will be added to the "train."

Go

- Acting as the "engine," move throughout the room, making "chugga-chugga" sounds and picking up one "car" (child) at a time, until one long train has been formed.
- The train then heads out the door!

Another Transition Idea

- Instead of becoming a train, become one long snake. Simply change the "chugga-chugga" to a hissing sound!

We're Going Out the Door

Ready

- How can leaving a room be fun? When there is a fun song involved!

Set

- Change these simple lyrics to match your situation.
- Once you have chosen the lyrics you want to use, teach them to the children.

Go

- The following verses are appropriate for leaving the classroom, moving down a hallway, and exiting an outside door.
- Sing the following to the tune of "The Farmer in the Dell."

> *We're going out the door.*
> *We're going out the door.*
> *Hi-ho, outside we go*
> *We're going out the door.*
>
> *We're walking down the hall.*
> *We're walking down the hall.*
> *Hi-ho, outside we go*
> *We're walking down the hall.*

- Use only the first verse for exiting outside.

A' Marching We Will Go

Ready

- Contrary to popular belief, gross motor skills do not automatically progress from an immature to a mature level of development.
- The fact is, motor skills must be taught and practiced just like other skills in early childhood. Otherwise, a child will remain at a low level of performance, possibly for life.
- Transitions to outside the classroom provide perfect opportunities for children to practice various locomotor (traveling) skills.

Set

- Teach the children the following song and explain that you are all going to sing it while marching from the classroom to wherever it is you are going.

Go

- Sing the following to the tune of "The Farmer in the Dell."

  A'marching we will go,
  A'marching we will go,
  Hi-ho, away we go
  A'marching we will go.

Another Transition Idea

- To practice other locomotor skills, simply change *marching to walking, jumping, hopping, or galloping.*
- Once all the children are able to skip (children generally acquire this skill at about 5½ years old), you can also add *skipping.*

Follow the Leader

Ready

- This traditional game is an excellent activity for transitions to outside the classroom.

Set

- If the children are not yet familiar with the rules of this game, simply explain that they are to copy the actions of one person, who is the leader of this game. In the beginning, you may need to act as the leader.

Go

- The first time you introduce this game, act as leader.
- To vary the actions you wish the children to mimic, keep the elements of movement (space, shape, time, force, flow, and rhythm) in mind.
- For example, you might choose to move in the following ways:

  - sideways (space)
  - in a straight, curving, or zigzag pathway (space)
  - in a rounded (pointed, angular) shape (space)
  - slowly or quickly (time)
  - lightly or strongly (force)
  - with pauses (flow)
  - marching or galloping (rhythm)

Another Transition Idea

- If you are focusing on a transportation theme, incorporate it into this activity by leading the children while pretending to be an airplane, to ride a horse, to drive a car, or to row a boat!

And Another Transition Idea

- If you are focusing on an animal theme, lead the children while pretending to be an elephant, eagle, stalking cat, dinosaur, or another animal of your choice.

Problem Solving

Ready

- When you use problem solving as part of a transition, you add this essential skill to children's learning experiences.
- Divergent problem solving is essential to both critical and creative thinking skills.
- In addition, children get another opportunity to use their imaginations and express themselves.

Set

- Explain to the children that you are going to ask them to move from the classroom to wherever they are going in some unusual, fun ways.
- Assure them that there are no wrong ways to move!

Go

- Challenge them to move in one of the following ways:

  - find a way using only one foot (or three body parts, etc.).
  - move in the most crooked (rounded, pointed) shape possible.
  - move in a sideways direction, using any method of locomotion except walking or running.
  - find a way to move that involves a preposition (for example, over, under, around, between, or through).
  - move at a low (high) level in space.

Another Transition Idea

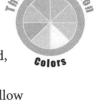

Colors

- Ask the children to move like something that is yellow (red, green, blue, etc.).
- Even more challenging: ask them to move *like* the color yellow (red, green, blue, etc.). You might read *My Many Colored Days* by Dr. Seuss to help with this concept.

And Another Transition Idea

Animals

- Challenge children to move like an animal found in the forest, found on a farm, that flies, that swims, or is found in a home.

Imagine!

Ready

- This activity also requires problem solving, but the emphasis here is on using imagination.

Set

- Discuss the following images so the children are familiar with them.

Go

- Challenge the children to move:

    - like water flowing
    - like an occupation (character, animal) they'd most like to be (have)
    - as through peanut butter (deep snow, waist-high water)
    - as on hot sand that is burning their feet

Another Transition Idea

- If you need to be especially quiet, as when going down a hallway past other classrooms, ask the children to pretend to move the same as one of the following:

  - turtles
  - weightless astronauts
  - butterflies
  - eagles
  - feathers
  - cats stalking their prey
  - clouds drifting through the sky
  - mimes

To the Library

Ready

- If you are leaving the classroom to visit the library (whether it is in the building or in another part of town), invite the children to move while pretending to be one of the images listed on the next page.

Set

● Discuss the suggestions below with the children before you ask them to act them out.

Go

● Challenge the children to move:

  ● in the shape of a book
  ● as a quiet librarian
  ● as a "bookworm"
  ● as a whisper

Row, Row, Row Your Boat

Ready

● The traditional verse of this song is perfect for a transportation theme, and for simply adding fun and familiarity to transitions.

Set

- If the children don't already know it, teach them to sing this old favorite.

Go

- As the children move in a single-file line, they can pretend to be rowing a boat.

> *Row, row, row your boat*
> *Gently down the stream.*
> *Merrily, merrily, merrily, merrily*
> *Life is but a dream!*

Another Transition Idea

- To continue with the transportation theme, vary the lyrics and movement accordingly. For example:

> *Paddle, paddle, paddle your canoe*
> *Gently down the stream.*
> *Merrily, merrily, merrily, merrily*
> *Life is but a dream!*

- Or try this one:

> *Drive, drive, drive your truck*
> *Gently down the road.*
> *Merrily, merrily, merrily, merrily*
> *Carrying your load!*

- Do the children know that walking is also a form of transportation? Help them understand that concept with the following lyrics:

> *Walk, walk, walk along*
> *Gently down the hall.*
> *Merrily, merrily, merrily, merrily*
> *Life is sure a ball!*

And Another Transition Idea

The Sea

- If you are exploring the concept of the sea with the children, use the following lyrics, accompanied by appropriate movements.

> *Swim, swim, swim along*
> *Gently in the sea.*
> *Merrily, merrily, merrily, merrily*
> *Take a look at me!*

- Or, another possibility:

> *Surf, surf, surf your board*
> *Gently toward the shore.*
> *Merrily, merrily, merrily, merrily*
> *Who wants to surf some more?*

High-Wire Act

Ready

Circus

- Most children—even those who have never been to one—are fascinated by the idea of the circus.
- Use that fascination to promote children's balancing skills, the concept of personal space, the ability to imagine, and to make another transition fun.

Set

- Talk to the children about various aspects of the circus, focusing on the tightrope walker.
- Ask them how they think the circus artist moves across the high wire. [Answer: By carefully placing one foot in front of the other and holding his arms out to the side.]
- Be sure the children realize that there is always a net below, just in case!

Go

- Line up the children in single file and invite them to imagine they are walking a tightrope out the door and to their destination! If necessary, remind them that tightrope walkers would not be touching anyone else as they cross the high wire.

What's the Weather?

Theme Connection
Weather

Ready

- Engage children's attention and imagination with the following weather-related images.

Set

- Talk with the children about these images. Ask them what comes to their minds when they think about the suggested images.

Go

- Invite the children to transition out of the classroom as though they were one of the following:

  - a gentle breeze
  - a snowflake
  - a sprinkling of rain
  - a drifting cloud
  - the sun shining!

- Remember that the children's interpretations may vary considerably, a positive sign that they feel free to be creative!

Nap or Rest Time

Relaxation is a learned skill. Today, with stress so much a part of our society and our children's lives, it is a greatly needed skill. Cherry (1981, Preface) says that relaxing can make serenity a part of children's lives, helping them learn "they can be in control of their own bodies and feelings rather than having to let their bodies and feelings control them." Jacobsen (1973), a leading authority in relaxation techniques, believes tension control can help children learn better.

Nap or rest time, in addition to offering rest and revitalization, provides a daily opportunity to help children acquire the skill of relaxation. By using imagery to promote relaxation, you enhance children's ability to imagine, a skill essential for problem solving and inventiveness. If you include music, you expose them to the world of quiet, peaceful music, a positive step in the direction of aesthetic awareness of music's beauty.

The activities found in this chapter are intended for the three different components of nap or rest time transition: transitioning from activity to inactivity as they move to their mats or cots (pages 100-105, "Soothing Imagery I" to "With Feeling"), achieving relaxation once on the mats or cots (pages 105-109, "Soothing Imagery III" to "A Sleeping Contest"), and the transition out of nap time (pages 109-117, "Counting Sheep" to "Countdown"). All of the relaxation activities can be used any time children need to wind down.

Chants and songs that use children's names are included in this chapter. Sing or say these, looking at each child individually, or as you move quietly from cot to cot. Although the songs in this section are intended for *you* to sing, once children are familiar with the lyrics and melodies, you can certainly invite them to sing them quietly to themselves as they lie on their cots or mats.

Finally, help children awaken by choosing one of the activities designed specifically for that purpose. Children can then go quietly to prepared learning centers or into a group led by a teacher doing quiet activities. Children have varying body rhythms, so they should be allowed 15 to 20 minutes following nap or rest time for quiet activities (Cherry, 1981). Those children still asleep after most of the children are up and about should be awakened gently.

Soothing Imagery I

Ready

- This activity stimulates the imagination, and the pretending gives children a reason to move *slowly*, which may not come naturally to them and requires much more control than moving quickly!

Set

- If necessary, discuss the images you plan to use with the children, to ensure that they are familiar with them.

Go

- Ask the children to move to their mats or cots as one of the following:

  - balloons deflating and coming down from the sky
  - wind-up toys (or the Energizer bunny) winding down
  - a feather floating to the ground
  - turtles moving
  - snails crawling
  - bears lumbering to their caves for hibernation

Another Transition Idea

- Ask the children to move like one of the following images to support a transportation theme:

  - hot-air balloons or airplanes coming in for a gentle landing
  - a train chugging slowly into the station
  - motorboats or cars running out of gas

Soothing Imagery II

Ready

- This activity also requires imagination.
- Here, however, instead of asking children to pretend to be something or someone else, you will be challenging them to imagine themselves in a variety of situations.

Set

- Talk to the children about these situations.
- Have they been in any of these situations?

Go

- Invite the children to move to their cots or mats as though:

  - moving through peanut butter or marshmallow fluff
  - gradually shrinking
  - swimming with long, easy strokes
  - walking through deep snow or sticky mud
  - slowly sinking

Instant Replay

Ready

- Like the previous activity, this provides practice both in using imagination and moving slowly.

Set

- Ask the children if they have ever seen instant replay on television, for instance, during a football or baseball game.
- Most often, instant replay is shown in slow motion, which is much slower than real-life movement.

Go

- Ask the children to move to their mats as though in slow-motion instant replay. They can also act out a scene along the way!

We're Getting So Tired

Ready

- Children love to sing and are always happy to express themselves.
- This activity offers them an opportunity to do both, *and* it gives them reason to move quietly and to look forward to resting.

Set

- Talk to the children about the concept of being "at our best" when rested.

Go

● Teach them the following song, sung to the tune of "On Top of Old Smokey." (Sing it alone until the children are familiar with it; with repetition, it won't be long before they join you.)

> *We're getting so tired*
> *It's time to lie down.*
> *We're glad it is naptime*
> *We won't make a sound.*
> *We're getting so tired.*
> *We can't wait to rest.*
> *And once we are rested,*
> *We'll be at our best.*

Another Transition Idea

● This is a wonderful opportunity to introduce children to the musical concept of *ritardando*, which refers to music that gradually slows down, and to help children with the control required to move slowly.
● All you have to do is start singing the above song at a moderate tempo and then slower and slower and slower, encouraging the children to match their movements to your tempo. (If you model this, they will get the idea.)

Slowing Down

Ready

● Slow or sustained movement is much more difficult for children than fast movement because it requires additional control.
● This activity will help children acquire the ability to move with control because it uses two senses, sight and hearing. The children will think it is a game!
● This activity is also an example of *ritardando*, defined in the previous activity.

Set

- Explain to the children that you are going to clap your hands or beat a drum slowly as they move to their mats or cots, and you want them to take nice, slow steps that match the hand claps or drumbeat.
- Demonstrate so they can see what you mean.

Go

- Walk at a slow to moderate tempo ahead of the children and clap your hands or beat the drum, taking one step per beat.
- Encourage the children to move as you do.
- Gradually slow both your claps or beats and steps.
- By the time you reach the mats or cots, your claps and steps should be very, very slow.

Another Transition Idea

- Eventually, the children should be able to do this to your rhythmic accompaniment only. In other words, you will not have to move with them.

With Feeling

Theme Connection
Self-Awareness

Ready

- Emotions, including the three listed underneath "Go" on the following page, have particular effects on the body.
- While the first activity usually tenses the body, the second two do the opposite by loosening up the body.
- This activity offers children the opportunity to express themselves in a safe environment *and* to experience the contrast between contracted and released muscles, which is important to the relaxation process.

Set

- Talk to the children about times they have felt the three emotions listed on the following page.
- Ask them how it made their bodies look and feel.
- Ask them to imagine how it would make their bodies move.

Go

- Ask the children to approach their mats or cots as though feeling the following, in this order:

  - very mad
  - very sad
  - very, very tired

Soothing Imagery III

Ready

- The imagery in this activity can be used once the children are lying on their mats, to help them relax.

Set

- If necessary, talk to the children about these images.
- What do they think these things would feel like?
- Which do they like best?

Go

- In a very quiet voice, ask the children to imagine they are:

  - floating on a cloud
  - soaking in a warm tub
  - lying on the beach, feeling the warm sun and cool breeze
  - drifting on a breeze
  - drifting off to sleep

I'm Melting...

Ready

- Every child is a scientist at heart, exploring and discovering new concepts every day.
- The process of melting fascinates children.
- This activity uses that fascination to inspire a relaxed state as children transition from moving around to inactivity.

Set

- Talk to the children about melting.
- Ask them:

  What are some things that melt?

  Is it a fast process, or does it take place slowly?

Go

- Once the children are at their mats or cots, ask them to show you what they would look like if they were one of the following things that melt:

  - ice cream
  - an ice cube
  - a snowperson
  - a stick of butter

Statues & Rag Dolls

Ready

- Contracting and releasing the muscles is an age-old relaxation technique, but those words mean nothing to young children.
- Use meaningful imagery to help children develop the ability to contract and release their muscles.

Set

- Talk with the children about statues and rag dolls.
- Ask the children:

  What do you think of when you imagine statues and rag dolls?

  What would it feel like to be a statue? A rag doll?

Go

- Once the children are lying on their mats, ask them to demonstrate, alternately, being a statue and a rag doll.
- Continue the pattern for awhile, always ending with the rag doll.

Being Balloons

Ready

- Some people prefer to relax using contraction and release of muscles; others have more success with deep breathing.
- This activity promotes the latter through its use of imagery that the children can relate to and will find fun.

Set

- Talk to the children about balloons slowly inflating and deflating. Better yet, if you have a balloon available, show them.
- Ask them what they think happens to the balloon as it is inflated, and then deflated?

Go

- Once the children are lying on their mats, ask them to imagine they are balloons, in any color they want.
- Now, invite them to pretend they are slowly inflating by breathing in slowly through the nose.
- Once fully inflated, they begin to slowly deflate by letting air out through the mouth.

Note: Repeat this exercise only once or twice; any more may induce hyperventilation.

Another Transition Idea

- This exercise can also be done in a standing position.
- Use it with the children *before* they move to their mats or just as they arrive at their mats.

Imagine!

Ready

- With so many ever-present, ready-made images available to children today via television, video, and computer, children have very little need to create images of their own.
- This activity will go a long way toward reversing this worrisome trend.

Set

- Ask the children to lie down and close their eyes.

Go

- Ask them to paint a picture—a restful one—in their minds. You might ask them to imagine they are at the beach, provided that is something they are likely to be familiar with.
- Can they feel the warm sun and the cool breeze and the blanket beneath them on the warm sand?
- What sounds can they hear? The waves rolling in? Seagulls overhead? Does it make them feel relaxed?

A Sleeping Contest

Ready

- This relaxation activity is appropriate for an especially competitive group of children.
- But, remember, there is never just one winner. *All* of the children are winners!

Set

- Use this activity once the children are lying on their mats or cots.

Go

- Challenge the children to show you who can sleep the soundest without snoring. If you don't add that last part, you are likely to end up with the walls vibrating!
- Once they are all demonstrating the appropriate response, tell them, in your quietest, nap or rest time voice that they are the best sleeping class you have ever seen.

Counting Sheep

Ready

- This activity offers children experience with counting and with using their imaginations.

Set

- Have the children ever heard the expression "counting sheep"?
- Explain that some people, when they have trouble falling asleep, close their eyes and imagine sheep jumping over a fence one at a time.
- Sing the song below very slowly to the tune of "Ten Little Indians."

Go

- Instruct the children to lie with their eyes closed, imagining the sheep.

> *One little,*
> *Two little,*
> *Three little sheep,*
> *Four little,*
> *Five little,*
> *Six little sheep,*
> *Seven little,*
> *Eight little,*
> *Nine little sheep,*
> *Helping us to sleep!*

Rest Your Eyes

Ready

- This activity will help children rest and relax.

Set

- Once the children have settled onto their mats or cots, you can sing this tune to each of them individually as you tiptoe from mat to mat.

Go

- Sing the following to the tune of Brahms' "Lullaby."
- The restful, quiet words are:

Rest your eyes.
Rest your eyes.
Rest your eyes, little [Nathan].
Let your body relax.
Feel the peace that it brings.

Spending Quiet Time

Ready

- Use this song to encourage children to lie down and rest.

Set

- If desired, first discuss with the children the concept that taking a nap or rest time each day is healthy and wise.

Go

- Sing the following to the tune of "Eensy-Weensy Spider."
- The restful words are:

Let's lie down on our mats now,
And rest our tired eyes.
Taking a daily nap
Is considered wise.
So take this time to lie back,
And let your muscles go.
'Cause spending quiet time each day
Is good for you, you know.

Sleepy, Sleepy

Ready

- The slower and quieter you sing this song, the more effective it will be.

Set

- You may want to talk to the children about what is meant by "heavy lids."

Go

- Sing the following to the tune of "Twinkle, Twinkle, Little Star."

> *Sleepy, sleepy, little kids*
> *Time to rest those heavy lids.*
> *Close your eyes and breathe real deep.*
> *Fall into a gentle sleep.*
> *Sleepy, sleepy, little kids*
> *Time to rest those heavy lids.*

It's Time to Rest Now

Ready

- This is a particularly good activity if children are having difficulty winding down.
- If you sing to children individually, rather than to the group as a whole, change the "we" to "you" in the lyrics.

Set

- This song is short enough so you can sing it to the group as a whole or to the children individually as you move from mat to mat.

Go

- Sing the following to the tune of "You Are My Sunshine."

> *It's time to rest now*
> *And have some quiet.*
> *To be silent for a while*

And once we're rested.
We will feel better,
And we'll get up with a smile.

Hush Little Children

Ready

- This song is appropriate for singing to the group as a whole.

Set

- Sing this song once the children are all settled on their mats.

Go

- Sing the following very softly to the tune of "Hush Little Baby."

> *Hush little children*
> *Rest a while.*
> *Dream the dreams*
> *That make you smile.*
> *Close your eyes*
> *And breathe a sigh.*
> *Fall asleep*
> *To this lullaby.*

Are You Sleeping?

Ready

- Children who are still asleep after most of the children are up and about should be woken *gently*.
- Use this little song as you move from one sleeping child to another.

Set

- Place a hand on the shoulder of each sleeping child as you quietly sing this song.

Go

- Sing the following to the tune of "Where Is Thumbkin?"
- Change the name each time you repeat the song.

Are you sleeping,
Are you sleeping,
Little [Clark],
Little [Clark]?
It is time to wake up.
Now's the time to wake up,
Little [Clark],
Little [Clark].

Time to Wake

Ready

- This activity tells children when nap or rest time is over.

Set

- Sing this song to alert the children that nap or rest time is at an end.

Go

- Sing the following to the tune of "Jingle Bells."

Time to wake,
Time to rise,
Time to move along.
Now that we have had a nap
Let's wake up to this song—
Oh!
Time to wake,
Time to rise,
Time to have some fun.
Now that we have had a nap
Let's get up, everyone!

Up Go the Children

Ready

- This song is appropriate to use as a signal that nap or rest time is ending.

Set

- Sing the lyrics softly and cheerfully.

Go

- Sing to the tune of "Pop Goes the Weasel."

> *Nap [rest] time now is at its end,*
> *All my favorite children.*
> *Time to wake and greet a friend*
> *Up go the children!*
>
> *So when you're ready, open eyes,*
> *Then sit and stretch, my children.*
> *Time to get some exercise,*
> *Up go the children!*

Wake Up, Wake Up

Ready

- Use this chant when it is time for children to begin waking up.

Set

- Recite these words *gently* and in an inviting tone.

Go

- The chant is as follows:

> *Wake up, wake up*
> *Open your eyes.*
> *Nap [rest] time has made us*
> *Healthy and wise.*
> *Wake up, wake up*
> *Nap [rest] time is done.*
> *It's time to get up*
> *And have some more fun!*

Waking Imagery

Ready

- This activity will be most successful if you have spoken to the children about the images before nap or rest time.

Set

- As the children are waking up, they might like to do some *pretending*.
- The following imagery idea can be used for that purpose.

Go

- Ask the children to wake and rise as though they are:

  - a bear coming out of hibernation
  - a cat waking and stretching
  - a baby chick emerging from an egg
  - a turtle poking out from its shell

Another Transition Idea

- Other images you can use include:

  - a butterfly emerging from its cocoon
  - a person waking up and stretching first thing in the morning

Countdown

Ready

- Children love to count down from 10 to 0.
- Use it here as the children begin to wake up.

Set

- Before using this activity, tell the children that they can "blast off" (get up) from their cots at the end of the countdown.

Go

- When you see that most of the children are ready to get up from nap or rest time, begin counting *slowly* back from 10.
- Follow "0" with "Up now."
- Children who want to can "blast off."

Departure

Achieving closure brings great satisfaction, so the transition to departure is second only in importance to arrival. A cheerful, successful transition to departure can help children feel good about their day, good about you, and good about returning in the morning or after the weekend.

Use one of the first activities in this chapter of *Teachable Transitions* to bring the children together at the end of the day. Once together, help the children begin to unwind by asking them to imagine they are snow sculptures, blocks of ice, or ice cream cones slowly melting to the ground. When everyone is on the floor, sing an uplifting song or do an activity that reviews what they experienced or learned during the day. There are suggestions for both in this chapter!

You will find activities to bring the children together at the end of the day on pages 120-125 ("1-2-3" to "The Train"). On pages 125-128 ("Punchinello" to "A Very Good Day") you will find activities you can use to help the children review a part of their day. And, at the end of this chapter on pages 128-135 ("This Is My Friend" to "Leave Like a..."), you will find activities to wrap up the day and bring a smile to the children's faces.

Then, just as each arriving child was welcomed individually, each departing child should be acknowledged individually. Choose one of the activities in this chapter that uses the children's names, or simply address the children by name before they leave.

The activities in this chapter will help bring closure to the day, provide a review of the day, and make children feel great!

1-2-3

Ready

- This is a simple chant you can use to bring children into a circle.

Set

- Before you use this activity for the first time, let the children know that they are to form a circle while you chant the verse below.
- Blink the lights off and on or use whatever signal the children are familiar with to get their attention.

Go

- Chant the following:

> 1-2-3,
> Let me see
> A beautiful circle
> As round as can be.

Circle, Circle

Ready

- Use this song to gather the children into a circle (standing or sitting).

Set

- The lyrics of this song make it evident to the children what you are expecting. Review the song and your expectations with them before using it.

Go

- Sing this to the tune of "Twinkle, Twinkle, Little Star."

> Circle, circle
> Nice and round
> Make one now
> Without a sound.

Stand [sit] together
On the floor.
Come together
Now and you're
In a circle
Nice and round
The most perfect
Circle found!

Come to the Center

Ready

- Use this song to bring children together in the circle time area, or wherever it is you typically gather.

Set

- Let the children know what you expect when you begin to sing this song.
- Tell them you expect them to be gathered together by the time the song ends.

Go

- Sing the following to the tune of "On Top of Old Smokey."

Please come to the center
Of the room right now.
Please do so quietly
I know you know how!

Please come to the center
And join me to say,
"Goodbye and I love you
It's been a great day!"

Tummy to Tummy

Ready

- Here is a problem-solving challenge to bring children into a circle.
- Before using this activity, be sure the children are ready to handle it cognitively!

Set

- Use an attention-getting signal with the class, such as turning off the lights, singing a song, or ringing a soft bell.

Go

- Challenge the children to make a round shape using everyone in the class.

Another Transition Idea

- When the children are developmentally ready, make this more challenging. Ask them to hold hands with each other and to stand so all of their tummies are facing the same spot.

Ring Around the Rosie

Ready

- This old favorite is played in the traditional manner. It is a fun, familiar activity to bring children together in a circle on the floor.

Set

- Use one of the previous activities or simply call the children together into a circle.
- Stand together, holding hands.

Go

- As you sing the first three lines of the song, circle around. The fourth line is self-explanatory!

> *Ring around the rosie*
> *A pocket full of posies*
> *Ashes, ashes*
> *We all fall down!*

Come to the Circle Area If...

Ready

- Bring the children to the circle area of the room with this activity that will get them thinking.

Set

- Before using this activity or its first alternative, be sure the children know the letters of their names and the months in which they were born.

Go

- Call out, "Come to the circle area if your first name begins with the letter [A]."
- Continue until all of the children are gathered together.

Another Transition Idea

- Substitute the children's birth months for the letters of their names. For example, call out, "Come to the circle area if your birthday is in January." Continue for all 12 months.
- Each time you do this, vary the order of the months.

And Another Transition Idea

- This variation requires the children to think about their responses *and* move to the circle area in a manner befitting their response.
- Call out "Come to the circle area if cats [dogs, horses, birds, or any other pet that children have] are your favorite animal."
- The children then move to the circle area *as* that animal.

The Train

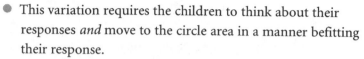

Ready

- This activity is especially appropriate when you are using a transportation theme.
- Trains fascinate children, so this two-part game will prove to be popular any time!
- Use it to bring the children together and to see them off individually.

Set

- Talk to the children about trains. How many children have traveled in a train?
- Explain the rules of this game. Designate one spot in the room as the train's final destination. The coatroom or the children's cubbies would be perfect.

Go

- As the children scatter about the room in the first part of this activity, circle around the room stopping near one child at a time and calling out, "Choo-choo. All aboard!"
- The child closest to you will then "board" the train by standing behind you and placing his hands on your waist.
- The train then continues around the room, picking up passengers in this manner, until all of the children are aboard.
- Continue to circle the classroom, stopping each time at the spot designated as the final train station.
- Each time you stop, one passenger departs. This can either be the first or last child in line. If it is the first, the "new" first child simply moves up and attaches to you.
- As each child departs, the rest chant, "Choo-choo. See you tomorrow, [Julia]."
- Continue until all of the passengers have reached their final destination!

Punchinello

Ready

- This is an excellent end-of-the-day activity that serves as a review of something learned or experienced.
- It also gives children an opportunity to make choices—so important to personal responsibility—and to express themselves.

Set

- The children form a circle with one child in the center ("Punchinello").

Go

- The children chant or sing:

    What can you do
    Punchinello, funny fellow?
    What can you do
    Punchinello, funny you?

- The child in the center chooses one of the day's activities to demonstrate.
- When he is through, the group sings:

    We can do it, too
    Punchinello, funny fellow.
    We can do it, too
    Punchinello, funny you!

- And they do! Each child, in turn, has a chance to be Punchinello.

The End of the Day

Ready

- This activity serves the same purpose as "Punchinello," but has the additional benefit of using the children's names.

Set

- The children sit on the floor in a circle.
- Ask one child at a time to go to the center of the circle, or address one child at a time, sequentially, around the circle.

Go

- Chant with the children:

    It's the end of the day
    Almost time to go.
    Tell us, [Sam],
    What do you know?

- The child called on demonstrates something learned during the day.
- If time permits, the rest of the children can replicate each response.

One Word

Ready

- This activity offers children an opportunity to explore descriptive language, to consider it as it relates to their experiences that day, and to express themselves physically.

Set

- Sit in a circle with the children and explain that each child will be asked to describe his day with *one word*.

Go

- Go around the circle and ask each child, in turn, to describe the day with just *one word*. Possible responses might include *busy, happy, fun, sunny,* or *snowy*.
- While still sitting, that child then demonstrates that word with his body. For example, if a child has responded *sunny*, he might "brighten" his body by sitting up straighter and smiling broadly.

A Very Good Day

Ready

- This activity is a musical review!
- There is nothing like a song to ensure a feel-good atmosphere.

Set

- Sit in a circle with the children.

Go

- Sing the following to the tune of "We Wish You a Merry Christmas."

We've had a very good day.
We've had a very good day.
We've had a very good day.
Now it's come to an end.

Let's talk about what we learned.
Let's talk about what we learned.
Let's talk about what we learned.
Let's talk friend to friend.

- Each child, in turn, then tells something he learned that day.
- Then sing the final verse:

It's been a very good day.
It's been a very good day.
It's been a very good day.
Can't wait to see you again!

This Is My Friend

Ready

- This game was introduced under "Arrival," but it is just as wonderful for saying goodbye as it is for saying hello.
- This departure version has two modifications.

Set

- Sit in a circle with the children, holding hands.

Go

- Raise the arm of the child to your right or left, saying, "This is my friend..."
- That child then says his name, holds up the arm of the next person in the circle, and repeats, "This is my friend..."
- That child says his name, and the process continues around the circle, in the same direction, until each child has introduced himself and all arms are in the air.
- The group then applauds for a job well done.

Another Transition Idea

- Once the children know one another's names, they introduce each other. For instance, Antonio might say, "This is my friend Amy" and raise the arm of the child to his left.
- After everyone has been introduced and all arms are in the air, everyone applauds.

We Have Had a Wonderful Day

Ready

- This simple song affirms that it has been a worthwhile day and reassures children that there will be another tomorrow!

Set

- Sit in a circle with the children.

Go

- Sing the following to the tune of "Twinkle, Twinkle, Little Star."

We have had a wonderful day.
We have worked and we have played.
Now we sing this goodbye song
'Cause it's time to say so long.
But we're not sad because we know
We'll be back here tomorrow.

We Wish You a Pleasant Evening

Ready

- This activity includes another feel-good song to sing with the group as a whole before departure.

Set

- Sit in a circle with the children.
- At first, you will sing this song on your own, but, after daily repetition, the children will know all the words and will happily join you.

Go

- Sing to the tune of "We Wish You a Merry Christmas."

> *We wish you a pleasant evening.*
> *We wish you a pleasant evening.*
> *We wish you a pleasant evening,*
> *And a most restful night.*
>
> *We'll see you in the morning.*
> *We'll see you in the morning.*
> *We'll see you in the morning,*
> *And it will be a delight!*

Time to Go

Ready

- Sing this song to the whole class or to each child individually as he is about to depart from the room.
- If you sing it to all of the children at once, say goodbye to one child at a time, using their names.

Set

- Sit in a circle with the children, with everyone singing the song together.

Go

- Sing the following to the tune of "Row, Row, Row Your Boat."

  Time, time, time to go.
  I hate to say goodbye.
  But we will soon meet again,
  And then we can say hi!

Another Transition Idea

- Once the children are familiar with the song, teach them to sing it in rounds!

It Was Good to Have You With Us

Ready

- This activity uses a chant for each departing child, one that enables use of each child's name.
- This is certain to make children feel special.

Set

- Use this chant as each child departs from the circle or as he is exiting the door.
- In either case, you can say it alone or accompanied by the children who remain.

Go

- The words to the chant are:

  It was good to have you with us today.
  It was good to have you, [Michael].
  It was good to have you with us today.
  I'll (we'll) see you in the morning (on Monday).

We'll See You Tomorrow

Ready

- Here is a song that uses the children's names.

Set

- Sing this song with all of the children, or the remaining children, as each child departs from the circle or as he is exiting the door.

Go

- Sing the following to the tune of "Goodnight, Ladies."

    Goodbye, [Collin]
    Goodbye, [Collin]
    Goodbye, [Collin]
    We'll (I'll) see you tomorrow (on Monday).

High-Five

Ready

- This is a fun fingerplay!

Set

- Stand in a circle with the children.

Go

- Chant the following, performing the actions appearing in parentheses next to each line.

    It's time to go (point to a wrist, where a watch would be)
    To say goodbye. (wave goodbye)
    It's been a great day. (display thumbs-up)
    So here's a high-five! (children raise both hands, palms facing out, and gently slap the palms of the children on either side of them)

- The children then pass you, one by one, with each one receiving an individual high-five.
- If a second adult is available, she or he can stand at the door to give each departing child another high-five!

If You're Happy

Ready

- This activity uses a familiar song.
- The first verse of this old favorite is performed in the traditional way, two new verses are added to make it a great departure activity.

Set

- Sit in a circle with the children.

Go

- Sing—and act out—the following:

If you're happy and you know it, clap your hands.
   (clap, clap)
If you're happy and you know it, clap your hands. (clap, clap)
If you're happy and you know it, then your face will surely show it. (smile)
If you're happy and you know it, clap your hands. (clap, clap)

If you're tired and you know it, give a yawn. (big yawn)
If you're tired and you know it, give a yawn. (big yawn)
If you're tired and you know it, then your face will surely show it. (drooping eyes)
If you're tired and you know it, give a yawn. (big yawn)

If you've had a good time today, shout hooray. ("Hooray!")
If you've had a good time today, shout hooray. ("Hooray!")
If you've had a good time today, and you want to come back and play. (Thumbs up!)
If you've had a good time today, shout hooray. ("Hooray!")

ABC Departure

Ready
- This activity is an alternative to dismissing children from the circle by name.

Set
- To add to the learning experience, post the alphabet in large block letters where all of the children can see it and you can easily point to the letters.

Go
- Point to a letter and tell the children that everyone whose first name begins with that letter is dismissed.
- You may start with A and work alphabetically to help the children learn their ABCs, but if you do it this way every time, the children will always be dismissed in the same order.
- To change this, you can either mix up the letters or you can sometimes use first names and sometimes last names.

Another Transition Idea

- Post the months of the year and dismiss children by their month of birth!

Leave Like a ...

Theme Connection

Animals

Ready
- This departure activity makes full use of the imagination.

Set
- Talk to the children about how each of the following animals moves, asking them to guess what they all have in common.
- The children may come up with some answers you had not considered, but, besides the fact that they are all animals, the point is that all of the animals' movements are *quiet*!

Go

- Dismiss the children one at a time or in small groups (everyone wearing the color blue, with brown hair, or any other characteristic), choosing one of the following images for each to portray as they depart:

  - a cat creeping
  - a bunny hopping
  - a mouse creeping
  - a giraffe moving
  - a butterfly fluttering
  - an eagle soaring

Another Transition Idea

- Other images that don't fall under the heading of animals but that are also quiet include:

  - a bubble floating
  - a feather floating
  - a glider airplane gliding

And Another Transition Idea

- Invite children to depart as something related to the season or to an upcoming holiday. Examples include a falling leaf, a snowflake, a seed sprouting, or a candle flickering.
- You may have to provide the examples at first, but eventually you will want to challenge them to come up with their own examples!

Theme Connection — Seasons

Theme Connection — Holidays & Celebrations

References

Allen, K. E., & B. Hart. 1984. *The early years: Arrangements for learning.* Englewood Cliffs, NJ: Prentice-Hall.

Beaty, J. J. 1984. *Skills for preschool teachers.* Columbus OH: Merrill.

Cherry, C. 1981. *Think of something quiet.* Carthage IL: Fearon.

Davidson, J. 1982. Wasted time: The ignored dilemma. In J. F. Brown, ed., *Curriculum planning for young children* (pp. 196-204). Washington DC: National Association for the Education of Young Children.

Essa, E. 1999. *Introduction to early childhood education.* Albany NY: Delmar.

Gordon, A., & K.W. Browne. 1996. *Beginnings and beyond, 4th ed.* Albany, NY: Delmar.

Hamilton, D. S., & B.M. Flemming. 1990. *Resources for creative teaching in early childhood education, 2nd ed.* Fort Worth TX: Harcourt Brace Jovanovich.

Hildebrand, V. 1980. *Guiding young children.* New York: Macmillan.

Isenberg, J. P., & M.R. Jalongo. 1997. *Creative expression and play in the early childhood curriculum.* New York: Merrill.

Jacobsen, E. 1973. *Teaching and learning new methods for old arts.* Chicago: National Foundation for Progressive Relaxation.

Orlick, T. 1978. *The cooperative sports and games book: Challenge without competition.* New York: Pantheon.

Pica, R. 2000. *Experiences in movement, 2nd ed.* Albany NY: Delmar.

Index

T

V

W

Creating Readers

Over 1000 Games, Activities, Tongue Twisters, Fingerplays, Songs, and Stories to Get Children Excited About Reading

Pam Schiller

Simple games and activities to help children learn the sound of every letter in the alphabet.

Learn the basic building blocks of reading with *Creating Readers,* the comprehensive resource that develops a strong foundation for pre-readers. *Creating Readers* gives teachers and parents the tools to teach pre-reading skills with over 1000 activities, games, fingerplays, songs, tongue twisters, poems, and stories for the letters of the alphabet. This invaluable resource develops the child's desire to read as well as the skills needed to begin reading. *Creating Readers* starts children ages 3 to 8 towards a future rich with books and reading. 448 pages. 2001.

ISBN 0-87659-258-2 / Gryphon House / 16375 / PB

Wiggle Giggle & Shake

200 Ways to Move and Learn

Rae Pica

Enhance your classroom with 200 movement-inspiring activities for children ages four to eight. Explore 38 popular classroom themes such as holidays, nature, animals, nutrition, and more. This book offers simple, practical, and fun movement activities and ideas grouped according to these popular themes. 192 pages. 2001.

ISBN 0-87659-244-2 Gryphon House / 19284 / PB

Available at your favorite bookstore, school supply store, or order from Gryphon House at 800.638.0928 or www.gryphonhouse.com.